C-171   CAREER EXAMINATION SERIES

This is your
PASSBOOK for...

Court Clerk

Test Preparation Study Guide
Questions & Answers

COPYRIGHT NOTICE

This book is SOLELY intended for, is sold ONLY to, and its use is RESTRICTED to individual, bona fide applicants or candidates who qualify by virtue of having seriously filed applications for appropriate license, certificate, professional and/or promotional advancement, higher school matriculation, scholarship, or other legitimate requirements of education and/or governmental authorities.

This book is NOT intended for use, class instruction, tutoring, training, duplication, copying, reprinting, excerption, or adaptation, etc., by:

1) Other publishers
2) Proprietors and/or Instructors of "Coaching" and/or Preparatory Courses
3) Personnel and/or Training Divisions of commercial, industrial, and governmental organizations
4) Schools, colleges, or universities and/or their departments and staffs, including teachers and other personnel
5) Testing Agencies or Bureaus
6) Study groups which seek by the purchase of a single volume to copy and/or duplicate and/or adapt this material for use by the group as a whole without having purchased individual volumes for each of the members of the group
7) Et al.

Such persons would be in violation of appropriate Federal and State statutes.

PROVISION OF LICENSING AGREEMENTS – Recognized educational, commercial, industrial, and governmental institutions and organizations, and others legitimately engaged in educational pursuits, including training, testing, and measurement activities, may address request for a licensing agreement to the copyright owners, who will determine whether, and under what conditions, including fees and charges, the materials in this book may be used them. In other words, a licensing facility exists for the legitimate use of the material in this book on other than an individual basis. However, it is asseverated and affirmed here that the material in this book CANNOT be used without the receipt of the express permission of such a licensing agreement from the Publishers. Inquiries re licensing should be addressed to the company, attention rights and permissions department.

All rights reserved, including the right of reproduction in whole or in part, in any form or by any means, electronic or mechanical, including photocopying, recording, or by any information storage and retrieval system, without permission in writing from the Publisher.

Copyright © 2024 by
National Learning Corporation

212 Michael Drive, Syosset, NY 11791
(516) 921-8888 • www.passbooks.com
E-mail: info@passbooks.com

PUBLISHED IN THE UNITED STATES OF AMERICA

PASSBOOK® SERIES

THE *PASSBOOK® SERIES* has been created to prepare applicants and candidates for the ultimate academic battlefield – the examination room.

At some time in our lives, each and every one of us may be required to take an examination – for validation, matriculation, admission, qualification, registration, certification, or licensure.

Based on the assumption that every applicant or candidate has met the basic formal educational standards, has taken the required number of courses, and read the necessary texts, the *PASSBOOK® SERIES* furnishes the one special preparation which may assure passing with confidence, instead of failing with insecurity. Examination questions – together with answers – are furnished as the basic vehicle for study so that the mysteries of the examination and its compounding difficulties may be eliminated or diminished by a sure method.

This book is meant to help you pass your examination provided that you qualify and are serious in your objective.

The entire field is reviewed through the huge store of content information which is succinctly presented through a provocative and challenging approach – the question-and-answer method.

A climate of success is established by furnishing the correct answers at the end of each test.

You soon learn to recognize types of questions, forms of questions, and patterns of questioning. You may even begin to anticipate expected outcomes.

You perceive that many questions are repeated or adapted so that you can gain acute insights, which may enable you to score many sure points.

You learn how to confront new questions, or types of questions, and to attack them confidently and work out the correct answers.

You note objectives and emphases, and recognize pitfalls and dangers, so that you may make positive educational adjustments.

Moreover, you are kept fully informed in relation to new concepts, methods, practices, and directions in the field.

You discover that you are actually taking the examination all the time: you are preparing for the examination by "taking" an examination, not by reading extraneous and/or supererogatory textbooks.

In short, this PASSBOOK®, used directedly, should be an important factor in helping you to pass your test.

COURT CLERK

DUTIES:
Court Clerks work in the Court of Claims; Supreme and County Courts in counties with two or more full-time County Court Judges or one full-time County Court Judge and combined annual filings of indictments and Supreme Court civil actions exceeding 650; Family Courts with two or more full-time Judges; and city- and district-level courts with six or more full-time Judges. Court Clerks serve as part clerks swearing witnesses, polling jurors, maintaining custody of exhibits and keeping court minutes in individual assignment system and other parts. Court Clerks also work in court offices where they supervise Court Assistants and other court personnel engaged in processing prisoner correspondence, reviewing calendaring decisions, motions for sufficiency and preference, and orders for conformance with decisions. Court Clerks may also supervise a full-time branch office of a court staffed by Court Assistants, be designated to act in the absence of the Chief Clerk or Commissioner of Jurors, and perform other related duties.

SUBJECT OF EXAMINATION
This written examination will be multiple-choice designed to assess knowledge of legal terminology, statutes, rules and procedures in effect in the New York State Unified Court System as set forth in:
1. Civil Practice Laws and Rules - Articles 1, 2, 3, 4, 5, 6, 9, 10, 11, 12, 20, 21, 22, 23, 24, 30, 32, 34, 40, 41, 42, 43, 44, 50, 52, 55, 63, 70, 78 and 80 and any other statutes, rules and court procedures referred to therein;
2. Criminal Procedure Law-Articles 1,10, 30, 100, 110, 120, 160, 170, 180, 190, 195, 200, 210, 216, 220, 260, 270, 280, 300, 310, 320, 330, 350, 360, 380, 390, 410, 420, 430, 500, 720, 725 and 730 and any other statutes, rules and court procedures referred to therein;
3. Penal Law - Articles 10, 55 and 80 and any other statutes, rules and court procedures referred to therein;
4. Family Court Act - Articles 1 (Parts 1, 5, 6, 7), 2, 3 (Parts 1, 2, 4, 5, 6, 7, 8), 4, 5, 5-B, 6, 7, 8, 10, and 11 and any other statutes, rules and court procedures referred to therein;
5. Other laws and statutes including:
    a. Uniform Rules for the New York State Trial Courts - Parts 200 (Sections 1-9), 202 (Sections 2, 3, 5, 6, 8, 9, 12,13, 21, 22, 26, 27, 28, 42, 44, 48, 56, 67), and 205 (Sections 2-5, 7-11, 14, 15, 17, 24-26, 29, 34-37, 42-44, 49, 51-53, 59, 62-66, 80, 81, 85)
    b. Real Property Actions and Proceedings Law - Article 7;
    c. Domestic Relations Law - Articles 3 (Section 15), 5-A
    d. Vehicle and Traffic Law - Sections 510, 511, 1192 and 1193.
    e. Mental Hygiene Law - Article 10

HOW TO TAKE A TEST

I. YOU MUST PASS AN EXAMINATION

A. *WHAT EVERY CANDIDATE SHOULD KNOW*

Examination applicants often ask us for help in preparing for the written test. What can I study in advance? What kinds of questions will be asked? How will the test be given? How will the papers be graded?

As an applicant for a civil service examination, you may be wondering about some of these things. Our purpose here is to suggest effective methods of advance study and to describe civil service examinations.

Your chances for success on this examination can be increased if you know how to prepare. Those "pre-examination jitters" can be reduced if you know what to expect. You can even experience an adventure in good citizenship if you know why civil service exams are given.

B. *WHY ARE CIVIL SERVICE EXAMINATIONS GIVEN?*

Civil service examinations are important to you in two ways. As a citizen, you want public jobs filled by employees who know how to do their work. As a job seeker, you want a fair chance to compete for that job on an equal footing with other candidates. The best-known means of accomplishing this two-fold goal is the competitive examination.

Exams are widely publicized throughout the nation. They may be administered for jobs in federal, state, city, municipal, town or village governments or agencies.

Any citizen may apply, with some limitations, such as the age or residence of applicants. Your experience and education may be reviewed to see whether you meet the requirements for the particular examination. When these requirements exist, they are reasonable and applied consistently to all applicants. Thus, a competitive examination may cause you some uneasiness now, but it is your privilege and safeguard.

C. *HOW ARE CIVIL SERVICE EXAMS DEVELOPED?*

Examinations are carefully written by trained technicians who are specialists in the field known as "psychological measurement," in consultation with recognized authorities in the field of work that the test will cover. These experts recommend the subject matter areas or skills to be tested; only those knowledges or skills important to your success on the job are included. The most reliable books and source materials available are used as references. Together, the experts and technicians judge the difficulty level of the questions.

Test technicians know how to phrase questions so that the problem is clearly stated. Their ethics do not permit "trick" or "catch" questions. Questions may have been tried out on sample groups, or subjected to statistical analysis, to determine their usefulness.

Written tests are often used in combination with performance tests, ratings of training and experience, and oral interviews. All of these measures combine to form the best-known means of finding the right person for the right job.

II. HOW TO PASS THE WRITTEN TEST

A. NATURE OF THE EXAMINATION

To prepare intelligently for civil service examinations, you should know how they differ from school examinations you have taken. In school you were assigned certain definite pages to read or subjects to cover. The examination questions were quite detailed and usually emphasized memory. Civil service exams, on the other hand, try to discover your present ability to perform the duties of a position, plus your potentiality to learn these duties. In other words, a civil service exam attempts to predict how successful you will be. Questions cover such a broad area that they cannot be as minute and detailed as school exam questions.

In the public service similar kinds of work, or positions, are grouped together in one "class." This process is known as *position-classification*. All the positions in a class are paid according to the salary range for that class. One class title covers all of these positions, and they are all tested by the same examination.

B. FOUR BASIC STEPS

1) Study the announcement

How, then, can you know what subjects to study? Our best answer is: "Learn as much as possible about the class of positions for which you've applied." The exam will test the knowledge, skills and abilities needed to do the work.

Your most valuable source of information about the position you want is the official exam announcement. This announcement lists the training and experience qualifications. Check these standards and apply only if you come reasonably close to meeting them.

The brief description of the position in the examination announcement offers some clues to the subjects which will be tested. Think about the job itself. Review the duties in your mind. Can you perform them, or are there some in which you are rusty? Fill in the blank spots in your preparation.

Many jurisdictions preview the written test in the exam announcement by including a section called "Knowledge and Abilities Required," "Scope of the Examination," or some similar heading. Here you will find out specifically what fields will be tested.

2) Review your own background

Once you learn in general what the position is all about, and what you need to know to do the work, ask yourself which subjects you already know fairly well and which need improvement. You may wonder whether to concentrate on improving your strong areas or on building some background in your fields of weakness. When the announcement has specified "some knowledge" or "considerable knowledge," or has used adjectives like "beginning principles of…" or "advanced … methods," you can get a clue as to the number and difficulty of questions to be asked in any given field. More questions, and hence broader coverage, would be included for those subjects which are more important in the work. Now weigh your strengths and weaknesses against the job requirements and prepare accordingly.

3) Determine the level of the position

Another way to tell how intensively you should prepare is to understand the level of the job for which you are applying. Is it the entering level? In other words, is this the position in which beginners in a field of work are hired? Or is it an intermediate or advanced level? Sometimes this is indicated by such words as "Junior" or "Senior" in the class title. Other jurisdictions use Roman numerals to designate the level – Clerk I, Clerk II, for example. The word "Supervisor" sometimes appears in the title. If the level is not indicated by the title, check the description of duties. Will you be working under very close supervision, or will you have responsibility for independent decisions in this work?

4) Choose appropriate study materials

Now that you know the subjects to be examined and the relative amount of each subject to be covered, you can choose suitable study materials. For beginning level jobs, or even advanced ones, if you have a pronounced weakness in some aspect of your training, read a modern, standard textbook in that field. Be sure it is up to date and has general coverage. Such books are normally available at your library, and the librarian will be glad to help you locate one. For entry-level positions, questions of appropriate difficulty are chosen – neither highly advanced questions, nor those too simple. Such questions require careful thought but not advanced training.

If the position for which you are applying is technical or advanced, you will read more advanced, specialized material. If you are already familiar with the basic principles of your field, elementary textbooks would waste your time. Concentrate on advanced textbooks and technical periodicals. Think through the concepts and review difficult problems in your field.

These are all general sources. You can get more ideas on your own initiative, following these leads. For example, training manuals and publications of the government agency which employs workers in your field can be useful, particularly for technical and professional positions. A letter or visit to the government department involved may result in more specific study suggestions, and certainly will provide you with a more definite idea of the exact nature of the position you are seeking.

III. KINDS OF TESTS

Tests are used for purposes other than measuring knowledge and ability to perform specified duties. For some positions, it is equally important to test ability to make adjustments to new situations or to profit from training. In others, basic mental abilities not dependent on information are essential. Questions which test these things may not appear as pertinent to the duties of the position as those which test for knowledge and information. Yet they are often highly important parts of a fair examination. For very general questions, it is almost impossible to help you direct your study efforts. What we can do is to point out some of the more common of these general abilities needed in public service positions and describe some typical questions.

1) General information

Broad, general information has been found useful for predicting job success in some kinds of work. This is tested in a variety of ways, from vocabulary lists to questions about current events. Basic background in some field of work, such as sociology or economics, may be sampled in a group of questions. Often these are principles which have become familiar to most persons through exposure rather than through formal training. It is difficult to advise you how to study for these questions; being alert to the world around you is our best suggestion.

2) Verbal ability

An example of an ability needed in many positions is verbal or language ability. Verbal ability is, in brief, the ability to use and understand words. Vocabulary and grammar tests are typical measures of this ability. Reading comprehension or paragraph interpretation questions are common in many kinds of civil service tests. You are given a paragraph of written material and asked to find its central meaning.

3) Numerical ability

Number skills can be tested by the familiar arithmetic problem, by checking paired lists of numbers to see which are alike and which are different, or by interpreting charts and graphs. In the latter test, a graph may be printed in the test booklet which you are asked to use as the basis for answering questions.

4) Observation

A popular test for law-enforcement positions is the observation test. A picture is shown to you for several minutes, then taken away. Questions about the picture test your ability to observe both details and larger elements.

5) Following directions

In many positions in the public service, the employee must be able to carry out written instructions dependably and accurately. You may be given a chart with several columns, each column listing a variety of information. The questions require you to carry out directions involving the information given in the chart.

6) Skills and aptitudes

Performance tests effectively measure some manual skills and aptitudes. When the skill is one in which you are trained, such as typing or shorthand, you can practice. These tests are often very much like those given in business school or high school courses. For many of the other skills and aptitudes, however, no short-time preparation can be made. Skills and abilities natural to you or that you have developed throughout your lifetime are being tested.

Many of the general questions just described provide all the data needed to answer the questions and ask you to use your reasoning ability to find the answers. Your best preparation for these tests, as well as for tests of facts and ideas, is to be at your physical and mental best. You, no doubt, have your own methods of getting into an exam-taking mood and keeping "in shape." The next section lists some ideas on this subject.

IV. KINDS OF QUESTIONS

Only rarely is the "essay" question, which you answer in narrative form, used in civil service tests. Civil service tests are usually of the short-answer type. Full instructions for answering these questions will be given to you at the examination. But in case this is your first experience with short-answer questions and separate answer sheets, here is what you need to know:

1) **Multiple-choice Questions**

Most popular of the short-answer questions is the "multiple choice" or "best answer" question. It can be used, for example, to test for factual knowledge, ability to solve problems or judgment in meeting situations found at work.

A multiple-choice question is normally one of three types—
- It can begin with an incomplete statement followed by several possible endings. You are to find the one ending which *best* completes the statement, although some of the others may not be entirely wrong.
- It can also be a complete statement in the form of a question which is answered by choosing one of the statements listed.

- It can be in the form of a problem – again you select the best answer.

Here is an example of a multiple-choice question with a discussion which should give you some clues as to the method for choosing the right answer:

When an employee has a complaint about his assignment, the action which will *best* help him overcome his difficulty is to
- A. discuss his difficulty with his coworkers
- B. take the problem to the head of the organization
- C. take the problem to the person who gave him the assignment
- D. say nothing to anyone about his complaint

In answering this question, you should study each of the choices to find which is best. Consider choice "A" – Certainly an employee may discuss his complaint with fellow employees, but no change or improvement can result, and the complaint remains unresolved. Choice "B" is a poor choice since the head of the organization probably does not know what assignment you have been given, and taking your problem to him is known as "going over the head" of the supervisor. The supervisor, or person who made the assignment, is the person who can clarify it or correct any injustice. Choice "C" is, therefore, correct. To say nothing, as in choice "D," is unwise. Supervisors have and interest in knowing the problems employees are facing, and the employee is seeking a solution to his problem.

2) True/False Questions

The "true/false" or "right/wrong" form of question is sometimes used. Here a complete statement is given. Your job is to decide whether the statement is right or wrong.

SAMPLE: A roaming cell-phone call to a nearby city costs less than a non-roaming call to a distant city.

This statement is wrong, or false, since roaming calls are more expensive.

This is not a complete list of all possible question forms, although most of the others are variations of these common types. You will always get complete directions for answering questions. Be sure you understand *how* to mark your answers – ask questions until you do.

V. RECORDING YOUR ANSWERS

Computer terminals are used more and more today for many different kinds of exams.

For an examination with very few applicants, you may be told to record your answers in the test booklet itself. Separate answer sheets are much more common. If this separate answer sheet is to be scored by machine – and this is often the case – it is highly important that you mark your answers correctly in order to get credit.

An electronic scoring machine is often used in civil service offices because of the speed with which papers can be scored. Machine-scored answer sheets must be marked with a pencil, which will be given to you. This pencil has a high graphite content which responds to the electronic scoring machine. As a matter of fact, stray dots may register as answers, so do not let your pencil rest on the answer sheet while you are pondering the correct answer. Also, if your pencil lead breaks or is otherwise defective, ask for another.

Since the answer sheet will be dropped in a slot in the scoring machine, be careful not to bend the corners or get the paper crumpled.

The answer sheet normally has five vertical columns of numbers, with 30 numbers to a column. These numbers correspond to the question numbers in your test booklet. After each number, going across the page are four or five pairs of dotted lines. These short dotted lines have small letters or numbers above them. The first two pairs may also have a "T" or "F" above the letters. This indicates that the first two pairs only are to be used if the questions are of the true-false type. If the questions are multiple choice, disregard the "T" and "F" and pay attention only to the small letters or numbers.

Answer your questions in the manner of the sample that follows:

32. The largest city in the United States is
    A. Washington, D.C.
    B. New York City
    C. Chicago
    D. Detroit
    E. San Francisco

1) Choose the answer you think is best. (New York City is the largest, so "B" is correct.)
2) Find the row of dotted lines numbered the same as the question you are answering. (Find row number 32)
3) Find the pair of dotted lines corresponding to the answer. (Find the pair of lines under the mark "B.")
4) Make a solid black mark between the dotted lines.

VI. BEFORE THE TEST

Common sense will help you find procedures to follow to get ready for an examination. Too many of us, however, overlook these sensible measures. Indeed, nervousness and fatigue have been found to be the most serious reasons why applicants fail to do their best on civil service tests. Here is a list of reminders:

- Begin your preparation early – Don't wait until the last minute to go scurrying around for books and materials or to find out what the position is all about.
- Prepare continuously – An hour a night for a week is better than an all-night cram session. This has been definitely established. What is more, a night a week for a month will return better dividends than crowding your study into a shorter period of time.
- Locate the place of the exam – You have been sent a notice telling you when and where to report for the examination. If the location is in a different town or otherwise unfamiliar to you, it would be well to inquire the best route and learn something about the building.
- Relax the night before the test – Allow your mind to rest. Do not study at all that night. Plan some mild recreation or diversion; then go to bed early and get a good night's sleep.
- Get up early enough to make a leisurely trip to the place for the test – This way unforeseen events, traffic snarls, unfamiliar buildings, etc. will not upset you.
- Dress comfortably – A written test is not a fashion show. You will be known by number and not by name, so wear something comfortable.

- Leave excess paraphernalia at home – Shopping bags and odd bundles will get in your way. You need bring only the items mentioned in the official notice you received; usually everything you need is provided. Do not bring reference books to the exam. They will only confuse those last minutes and be taken away from you when in the test room.
- Arrive somewhat ahead of time – If because of transportation schedules you must get there very early, bring a newspaper or magazine to take your mind off yourself while waiting.
- Locate the examination room – When you have found the proper room, you will be directed to the seat or part of the room where you will sit. Sometimes you are given a sheet of instructions to read while you are waiting. Do not fill out any forms until you are told to do so; just read them and be prepared.
- Relax and prepare to listen to the instructions
- If you have any physical problem that may keep you from doing your best, be sure to tell the test administrator. If you are sick or in poor health, you really cannot do your best on the exam. You can come back and take the test some other time.

VII. AT THE TEST

The day of the test is here and you have the test booklet in your hand. The temptation to get going is very strong. Caution! There is more to success than knowing the right answers. You must know how to identify your papers and understand variations in the type of short-answer question used in this particular examination. Follow these suggestions for maximum results from your efforts:

1) Cooperate with the monitor

The test administrator has a duty to create a situation in which you can be as much at ease as possible. He will give instructions, tell you when to begin, check to see that you are marking your answer sheet correctly, and so on. He is not there to guard you, although he will see that your competitors do not take unfair advantage. He wants to help you do your best.

2) Listen to all instructions

Don't jump the gun! Wait until you understand all directions. In most civil service tests you get more time than you need to answer the questions. So don't be in a hurry. Read each word of instructions until you clearly understand the meaning. Study the examples, listen to all announcements and follow directions. Ask questions if you do not understand what to do.

3) Identify your papers

Civil service exams are usually identified by number only. You will be assigned a number; you must not put your name on your test papers. Be sure to copy your number correctly. Since more than one exam may be given, copy your exact examination title.

4) Plan your time

Unless you are told that a test is a "speed" or "rate of work" test, speed itself is usually not important. Time enough to answer all the questions will be provided, but this does not mean that you have all day. An overall time limit has been set. Divide the total time (in minutes) by the number of questions to determine the approximate time you have for each question.

5) Do not linger over difficult questions

If you come across a difficult question, mark it with a paper clip (useful to have along) and come back to it when you have been through the booklet. One caution if you do this – be sure to skip a number on your answer sheet as well. Check often to be sure that you have not lost your place and that you are marking in the row numbered the same as the question you are answering.

6) Read the questions

Be sure you know what the question asks! Many capable people are unsuccessful because they failed to *read* the questions correctly.

7) Answer all questions

Unless you have been instructed that a penalty will be deducted for incorrect answers, it is better to guess than to omit a question.

8) Speed tests

It is often better NOT to guess on speed tests. It has been found that on timed tests people are tempted to spend the last few seconds before time is called in marking answers at random – without even reading them – in the hope of picking up a few extra points. To discourage this practice, the instructions may warn you that your score will be "corrected" for guessing. That is, a penalty will be applied. The incorrect answers will be deducted from the correct ones, or some other penalty formula will be used.

9) Review your answers

If you finish before time is called, go back to the questions you guessed or omitted to give them further thought. Review other answers if you have time.

10) Return your test materials

If you are ready to leave before others have finished or time is called, take ALL your materials to the monitor and leave quietly. Never take any test material with you. The monitor can discover whose papers are not complete, and taking a test booklet may be grounds for disqualification.

VIII. EXAMINATION TECHNIQUES

1) Read the general instructions carefully. These are usually printed on the first page of the exam booklet. As a rule, these instructions refer to the timing of the examination; the fact that you should not start work until the signal and must stop work at a signal, etc. If there are any *special* instructions, such as a choice of questions to be answered, make sure that you note this instruction carefully.

2) When you are ready to start work on the examination, that is as soon as the signal has been given, read the instructions to each question booklet, underline any key words or phrases, such as *least, best, outline, describe* and the like. In this way you will tend to answer as requested rather than discover on reviewing your paper that you *listed without describing*, that you selected the *worst* choice rather than the *best* choice, etc.

3) If the examination is of the objective or multiple-choice type – that is, each question will also give a series of possible answers: A, B, C or D, and you are called upon to select the best answer and write the letter next to that answer on your answer paper – it is advisable to start answering each question in turn. There may be anywhere from 50 to 100 such questions in the three or four hours allotted and you can see how much time would be taken if you read through all the questions before beginning to answer any. Furthermore, if you come across a question or group of questions which you know would be difficult to answer, it would undoubtedly affect your handling of all the other questions.

4) If the examination is of the essay type and contains but a few questions, it is a moot point as to whether you should read all the questions before starting to answer any one. Of course, if you are given a choice – say five out of seven and the like – then it is essential to read all the questions so you can eliminate the two that are most difficult. If, however, you are asked to answer all the questions, there may be danger in trying to answer the easiest one first because you may find that you will spend too much time on it. The best technique is to answer the first question, then proceed to the second, etc.

5) Time your answers. Before the exam begins, write down the time it started, then add the time allowed for the examination and write down the time it must be completed, then divide the time available somewhat as follows:
   - If 3-1/2 hours are allowed, that would be 210 minutes. If you have 80 objective-type questions, that would be an average of 2-1/2 minutes per question. Allow yourself no more than 2 minutes per question, or a total of 160 minutes, which will permit about 50 minutes to review.
   - If for the time allotment of 210 minutes there are 7 essay questions to answer, that would average about 30 minutes a question. Give yourself only 25 minutes per question so that you have about 35 minutes to review.

6) The most important instruction is to *read each question* and make sure you know what is wanted. The second most important instruction is to *time yourself properly* so that you answer every question. The third most important instruction is to *answer every question*. Guess if you have to but include something for each question. Remember that you will receive no credit for a blank and will probably receive some credit if you write something in answer to an essay question. If you guess a letter – say "B" for a multiple-choice question – you may have guessed right. If you leave a blank as an answer to a multiple-choice question, the examiners may respect your feelings but it will not add a point to your score. Some exams may penalize you for wrong answers, so in such cases *only*, you may not want to guess unless you have some basis for your answer.

7) Suggestions
   a. Objective-type questions
      1. Examine the question booklet for proper sequence of pages and questions
      2. Read all instructions carefully
      3. Skip any question which seems too difficult; return to it after all other questions have been answered
      4. Apportion your time properly; do not spend too much time on any single question or group of questions

5. Note and underline key words – *all, most, fewest, least, best, worst, same, opposite,* etc.
6. Pay particular attention to negatives
7. Note unusual option, e.g., unduly long, short, complex, different or similar in content to the body of the question
8. Observe the use of "hedging" words – *probably, may, most likely,* etc.
9. Make sure that your answer is put next to the same number as the question
10. Do not second-guess unless you have good reason to believe the second answer is definitely more correct
11. Cross out original answer if you decide another answer is more accurate; do not erase until you are ready to hand your paper in
12. Answer all questions; guess unless instructed otherwise
13. Leave time for review

   b. Essay questions
     1. Read each question carefully
     2. Determine exactly what is wanted. Underline key words or phrases.
     3. Decide on outline or paragraph answer
     4. Include many different points and elements unless asked to develop any one or two points or elements
     5. Show impartiality by giving pros and cons unless directed to select one side only
     6. Make and write down any assumptions you find necessary to answer the questions
     7. Watch your English, grammar, punctuation and choice of words
     8. Time your answers; don't crowd material

8) Answering the essay question

Most essay questions can be answered by framing the specific response around several key words or ideas. Here are a few such key words or ideas:

M's: manpower, materials, methods, money, management
P's: purpose, program, policy, plan, procedure, practice, problems, pitfalls, personnel, public relations
   a. Six basic steps in handling problems:
     1. Preliminary plan and background development
     2. Collect information, data and facts
     3. Analyze and interpret information, data and facts
     4. Analyze and develop solutions as well as make recommendations
     5. Prepare report and sell recommendations
     6. Install recommendations and follow up effectiveness

   b. Pitfalls to avoid
     1. *Taking things for granted* – A statement of the situation does not necessarily imply that each of the elements is necessarily true; for example, a complaint may be invalid and biased so that all that can be taken for granted is that a complaint has been registered

2. *Considering only one side of a situation* – Wherever possible, indicate several alternatives and then point out the reasons you selected the best one
3. *Failing to indicate follow up* – Whenever your answer indicates action on your part, make certain that you will take proper follow-up action to see how successful your recommendations, procedures or actions turn out to be
4. *Taking too long in answering any single question* – Remember to time your answers properly

IX. AFTER THE TEST

Scoring procedures differ in detail among civil service jurisdictions although the general principles are the same. Whether the papers are hand-scored or graded by machine we have described, they are nearly always graded by number. That is, the person who marks the paper knows only the number – never the name – of the applicant. Not until all the papers have been graded will they be matched with names. If other tests, such as training and experience or oral interview ratings have been given, scores will be combined. Different parts of the examination usually have different weights. For example, the written test might count 60 percent of the final grade, and a rating of training and experience 40 percent. In many jurisdictions, veterans will have a certain number of points added to their grades.

After the final grade has been determined, the names are placed in grade order and an eligible list is established. There are various methods for resolving ties between those who get the same final grade – probably the most common is to place first the name of the person whose application was received first. Job offers are made from the eligible list in the order the names appear on it. You will be notified of your grade and your rank as soon as all these computations have been made. This will be done as rapidly as possible.

People who are found to meet the requirements in the announcement are called "eligibles." Their names are put on a list of eligible candidates. An eligible's chances of getting a job depend on how high he stands on this list and how fast agencies are filling jobs from the list.

When a job is to be filled from a list of eligibles, the agency asks for the names of people on the list of eligibles for that job. When the civil service commission receives this request, it sends to the agency the names of the three people highest on this list. Or, if the job to be filled has specialized requirements, the office sends the agency the names of the top three persons who meet these requirements from the general list.

The appointing officer makes a choice from among the three people whose names were sent to him. If the selected person accepts the appointment, the names of the others are put back on the list to be considered for future openings.

That is the rule in hiring from all kinds of eligible lists, whether they are for typist, carpenter, chemist, or something else. For every vacancy, the appointing officer has his choice of any one of the top three eligibles on the list. This explains why the person whose name is on top of the list sometimes does not get an appointment when some of the persons lower on the list do. If the appointing officer chooses the second or third eligible, the No. 1 eligible does not get a job at once, but stays on the list until he is appointed or the list is terminated.

X. HOW TO PASS THE INTERVIEW TEST

The examination for which you applied requires an oral interview test. You have already taken the written test and you are now being called for the interview test – the final part of the formal examination.

You may think that it is not possible to prepare for an interview test and that there are no procedures to follow during an interview. Our purpose is to point out some things you can do in advance that will help you and some good rules to follow and pitfalls to avoid while you are being interviewed.

What is an interview supposed to test?

The written examination is designed to test the technical knowledge and competence of the candidate; the oral is designed to evaluate intangible qualities, not readily measured otherwise, and to establish a list showing the relative fitness of each candidate – as measured against his competitors – for the position sought. Scoring is not on the basis of "right" and "wrong," but on a sliding scale of values ranging from "not passable" to "outstanding." As a matter of fact, it is possible to achieve a relatively low score without a single "incorrect" answer because of evident weakness in the qualities being measured.

Occasionally, an examination may consist entirely of an oral test – either an individual or a group oral. In such cases, information is sought concerning the technical knowledges and abilities of the candidate, since there has been no written examination for this purpose. More commonly, however, an oral test is used to supplement a written examination.

Who conducts interviews?

The composition of oral boards varies among different jurisdictions. In nearly all, a representative of the personnel department serves as chairman. One of the members of the board may be a representative of the department in which the candidate would work. In some cases, "outside experts" are used, and, frequently, a businessman or some other representative of the general public is asked to serve. Labor and management or other special groups may be represented. The aim is to secure the services of experts in the appropriate field.

However the board is composed, it is a good idea (and not at all improper or unethical) to ascertain in advance of the interview who the members are and what groups they represent. When you are introduced to them, you will have some idea of their backgrounds and interests, and at least you will not stutter and stammer over their names.

What should be done before the interview?

While knowledge about the board members is useful and takes some of the surprise element out of the interview, there is other preparation which is more substantive. It *is* possible to prepare for an oral interview – in several ways:

1) Keep a copy of your application and review it carefully before the interview

This may be the only document before the oral board, and the starting point of the interview. Know what education and experience you have listed there, and the sequence and dates of all of it. Sometimes the board will ask you to review the highlights of your experience for them; you should not have to hem and haw doing it.

2) Study the class specification and the examination announcement

Usually, the oral board has one or both of these to guide them. The qualities, characteristics or knowledges required by the position sought are stated in these documents. They offer valuable clues as to the nature of the oral interview. For example, if the job involves supervisory responsibilities, the announcement will usually indicate that knowledge of modern supervisory methods and the qualifications of the candidate as a supervisor will be tested. If so, you can expect such questions, frequently in the form of a hypothetical situation which you are expected to solve. NEVER go into an oral without knowledge of the duties and responsibilities of the job you seek.

3) Think through each qualification required

Try to visualize the kind of questions you would ask if you were a board member. How well could you answer them? Try especially to appraise your own knowledge and background in each area, *measured against the job sought*, and identify any areas in which you are weak. Be critical and realistic – do not flatter yourself.

4) Do some general reading in areas in which you feel you may be weak

For example, if the job involves supervision and your past experience has NOT, some general reading in supervisory methods and practices, particularly in the field of human relations, might be useful. Do NOT study agency procedures or detailed manuals. The oral board will be testing your understanding and capacity, not your memory.

5) Get a good night's sleep and watch your general health and mental attitude

You will want a clear head at the interview. Take care of a cold or any other minor ailment, and of course, no hangovers.

What should be done on the day of the interview?

Now comes the day of the interview itself. Give yourself plenty of time to get there. Plan to arrive somewhat ahead of the scheduled time, particularly if your appointment is in the fore part of the day. If a previous candidate fails to appear, the board might be ready for you a bit early. By early afternoon an oral board is almost invariably behind schedule if there are many candidates, and you may have to wait. Take along a book or magazine to read, or your application to review, but leave any extraneous material in the waiting room when you go in for your interview. In any event, relax and compose yourself.

The matter of dress is important. The board is forming impressions about you – from your experience, your manners, your attitude, and your appearance. Give your personal appearance careful attention. Dress your best, but not your flashiest. Choose conservative, appropriate clothing, and be sure it is immaculate. This is a business interview, and your appearance should indicate that you regard it as such. Besides, being well groomed and properly dressed will help boost your confidence.

Sooner or later, someone will call your name and escort you into the interview room. *This is it.* From here on you are on your own. It is too late for any more preparation. But remember, you asked for this opportunity to prove your fitness, and you are here because your request was granted.

What happens when you go in?

The usual sequence of events will be as follows: The clerk (who is often the board stenographer) will introduce you to the chairman of the oral board, who will introduce you to the other members of the board. Acknowledge the introductions before you sit down. Do not be surprised if you find a microphone facing you or a stenotypist sitting by. Oral interviews are usually recorded in the event of an appeal or other review.

Usually the chairman of the board will open the interview by reviewing the highlights of your education and work experience from your application – primarily for the benefit of the other members of the board, as well as to get the material into the record. Do not interrupt or comment unless there is an error or significant misinterpretation; if that is the case, do not hesitate. But do not quibble about insignificant matters. Also, he will usually ask you some question about your education, experience or your present job – partly to get you to start talking and to establish the interviewing "rapport." He may start the actual questioning, or turn it over to one of the other members. Frequently, each member undertakes the questioning on a particular area, one in which he is perhaps most competent, so you can expect each member to participate in the examination. Because time is limited, you may also expect some rather abrupt switches in the direction the questioning takes, so do not be upset by it. Normally, a board member will not pursue a single line of questioning unless he discovers a particular strength or weakness.

After each member has participated, the chairman will usually ask whether any member has any further questions, then will ask you if you have anything you wish to add. Unless you are expecting this question, it may floor you. Worse, it may start you off on an extended, extemporaneous speech. The board is not usually seeking more information. The question is principally to offer you a last opportunity to present further qualifications or to indicate that you have nothing to add. So, if you feel that a significant qualification or characteristic has been overlooked, it is proper to point it out in a sentence or so. Do not compliment the board on the thoroughness of their examination – they have been sketchy, and you know it. If you wish, merely say, "No thank you, I have nothing further to add." This is a point where you can "talk yourself out" of a good impression or fail to present an important bit of information. Remember, *you close the interview yourself*.

The chairman will then say, "That is all, Mr. _____, thank you." Do not be startled; the interview is over, and quicker than you think. Thank him, gather your belongings and take your leave. Save your sigh of relief for the other side of the door.

How to put your best foot forward

Throughout this entire process, you may feel that the board individually and collectively is trying to pierce your defenses, seek out your hidden weaknesses and embarrass and confuse you. Actually, this is not true. They are obliged to make an appraisal of your qualifications for the job you are seeking, and they want to see you in your best light. Remember, they must interview all candidates and a non-cooperative candidate may become a failure in spite of their best efforts to bring out his qualifications. Here are 15 suggestions that will help you:

1) Be natural – Keep your attitude confident, not cocky

If you are not confident that you can do the job, do not expect the board to be. Do not apologize for your weaknesses, try to bring out your strong points. The board is interested in a positive, not negative, presentation. Cockiness will antagonize any board member and make him wonder if you are covering up a weakness by a false show of strength.

2) Get comfortable, but don't lounge or sprawl

Sit erectly but not stiffly. A careless posture may lead the board to conclude that you are careless in other things, or at least that you are not impressed by the importance of the occasion. Either conclusion is natural, even if incorrect. Do not fuss with your clothing, a pencil or an ashtray. Your hands may occasionally be useful to emphasize a point; do not let them become a point of distraction.

3) Do not wisecrack or make small talk

This is a serious situation, and your attitude should show that you consider it as such. Further, the time of the board is limited – they do not want to waste it, and neither should you.

4) Do not exaggerate your experience or abilities

In the first place, from information in the application or other interviews and sources, the board may know more about you than you think. Secondly, you probably will not get away with it. An experienced board is rather adept at spotting such a situation, so do not take the chance.

5) If you know a board member, do not make a point of it, yet do not hide it

Certainly you are not fooling him, and probably not the other members of the board. Do not try to take advantage of your acquaintanceship – it will probably do you little good.

6) Do not dominate the interview

Let the board do that. They will give you the clues – do not assume that you have to do all the talking. Realize that the board has a number of questions to ask you, and do not try to take up all the interview time by showing off your extensive knowledge of the answer to the first one.

7) Be attentive

You only have 20 minutes or so, and you should keep your attention at its sharpest throughout. When a member is addressing a problem or question to you, give him your undivided attention. Address your reply principally to him, but do not exclude the other board members.

8) Do not interrupt

A board member may be stating a problem for you to analyze. He will ask you a question when the time comes. Let him state the problem, and wait for the question.

9) Make sure you understand the question

Do not try to answer until you are sure what the question is. If it is not clear, restate it in your own words or ask the board member to clarify it for you. However, do not haggle about minor elements.

10) Reply promptly but not hastily

A common entry on oral board rating sheets is "candidate responded readily," or "candidate hesitated in replies." Respond as promptly and quickly as you can, but do not jump to a hasty, ill-considered answer.

11) Do not be peremptory in your answers

A brief answer is proper – but do not fire your answer back. That is a losing game from your point of view. The board member can probably ask questions much faster than you can answer them.

12) Do not try to create the answer you think the board member wants

He is interested in what kind of mind you have and how it works – not in playing games. Furthermore, he can usually spot this practice and will actually grade you down on it.

13) Do not switch sides in your reply merely to agree with a board member

Frequently, a member will take a contrary position merely to draw you out and to see if you are willing and able to defend your point of view. Do not start a debate, yet do not surrender a good position. If a position is worth taking, it is worth defending.

14) Do not be afraid to admit an error in judgment if you are shown to be wrong

The board knows that you are forced to reply without any opportunity for careful consideration. Your answer may be demonstrably wrong. If so, admit it and get on with the interview.

15) Do not dwell at length on your present job

The opening question may relate to your present assignment. Answer the question but do not go into an extended discussion. You are being examined for a *new* job, not your present one. As a matter of fact, try to phrase ALL your answers in terms of the job for which you are being examined.

Basis of Rating

Probably you will forget most of these "do's" and "don'ts" when you walk into the oral interview room. Even remembering them all will not ensure you a passing grade. Perhaps you did not have the qualifications in the first place. But remembering them will help you to put your best foot forward, without treading on the toes of the board members.

Rumor and popular opinion to the contrary notwithstanding, an oral board wants you to make the best appearance possible. They know you are under pressure – but they also want to see how you respond to it as a guide to what your reaction would be under the pressures of the job you seek. They will be influenced by the degree of poise you display, the personal traits you show and the manner in which you respond.

ABOUT THIS BOOK

This book contains tests divided into Examination Sections. Go through each test, answering every question in the margin. We have also attached a sample answer sheet at the back of the book that can be removed and used. At the end of each test look at the answer key and check your answers. On the ones you got wrong, look at the right answer choice and learn. Do not fill in the answers first. Do not memorize the questions and answers, but understand the answer and principles involved. On your test, the questions will likely be different from the samples. Questions are changed and new ones added. If you understand these past questions you should have success with any changes that arise. Tests may consist of several types of questions. We have additional books on each subject should more study be advisable or necessary for you. Finally, the more you study, the better prepared you will be. This book is intended to be the last thing you study before you walk into the examination room. Prior study of relevant texts is also recommended. NLC publishes some of these in our Fundamental Series. Knowledge and good sense are important factors in passing your exam. Good luck also helps. So now study this Passbook, absorb the material contained within and take that knowledge into the examination. Then do your best to pass that exam.

EXAMINATION SECTION

EXAMINATION SECTION
TEST 1

DIRECTIONS: Each question or incomplete statement is followed by several suggested answers or completions. Select the one that BEST answers the question or completes the statement. *PRINT THE LETTER OF THE CORRECT ANSWER IN THE SPACE AT THE RIGHT.*

1. Which statement about the Rules from the CPLR is CORRECT? 1._____
   A. Any rule may be adopted.
   B. Any rule may be rescinded.
   C. Additional civil practice rules may be adopted, not inconsistent with the Constitution, by act of the legislature.
   D. All of the above

2. All civil judicial proceedings shall be prosecuted in the form of a(n) 2._____
   A. action
   B. special proceeding
   C. action except where prosecution in the form of a special proceeding is authorized
   D. mediation

3. The word *infant* as used in these rules means a person who has not attained the age of _____ years. 3._____
   A. 16   B. 17   C. 18   D. 21

4. An action for which no limitation is specifically prescribed by law must be commenced within _____ years. 4._____
   A. 4   B. 6   C. 10   D. 20

5. Proof of service shall NOT specify 5._____
   A. the papers served
   B. the person who was served
   C. the date, time, address or, in the event there is no address, place and manner of service
   D. witnesses who will be present

6. The court shall not stay or dismiss any action on the ground of inconvenient forum, where the action arises out of or relates to a 6._____
   A. contract, agreement or undertaking, and the parties to the contract have agreed that the law of this state shall govern their rights or duties in whole or in part
   B. tort, and the parties have agreed that the law of this state shall govern their rights or duties in whole or in part
   C. personal injury matter
   D. part civil and part criminal matter

7. Which of the following is NOT a prerequisite to a class action?
   A. The class is so numerous that joinder of all members, whether otherwise required for permitted, is impracticable.
   B. There are questions of law or fact common to the class which predominate over any questions affecting only individual members.
   C. The claims or defenses of the representative parties are typical of the claims or defenses of the class.
   D. A class action is inferior to other available methods for the fair and efficient adjudication of the controversy.

8. Which of the following situations is descriptive of a time when parties need NOT be joined?
   A. When the plaintiff has another effective remedy in case the action is dismissed on account of the nonjoinder
   B. When prejudice may not in the future be avoided
   C. The non-feasibility of a protective provision by order of the court or in the judgment
   D. When an effective judgment may not be rendered in the absence of the person who is not joined

9. A motion to proceed as a poor person need NOT include a(n)
   A. affidavit   B. certificate   C. notice   D. fee

10. A guardian ad litem may NOT be suggested to the court by
    A. an infant party if he is more than fourteen years of age
    B. a relative, friend or a guardian, committee of the property, or conservator
    C. any person not a party to the action
    D. any other party to the action if a motion has not been made under paragraph one or two within ten days after completion of service

11. Which of the following professionals may NOT file an affirmation in lieu of and with the same force and effect as an affidavit?
    A. Physician   B. Osteopath   C. Dentist   D. Psychologist

12. A notice of motion and supporting affidavits shall be served AT LEAST _____ days before the time at which the motion is noticed to be heard.
    A. six   B. seven   C. eight   D. ten

13. Answering affidavits shall be served AT LEAST _____ day(s) before the motion is noticed to be heard.
    A. one   B. two   C. three   D. four

14. Answering affidavits and any notice of cross-motion, with supporting papers, if any, shall be served AT LEAST _____ days before the motion is noticed to be heard if a notice served AT LEAST _____ days before such time so demands.
    A. seven; fifteen   B. seven; sixteen
    C. eight; fifteen   D. eight; sixteen

15. Failure to comply with a subpoena issued by any of the following EXCEPT _____ shall be punishable as a contempt of court.
    A. judge
    B. clerk
    C. officer of the court
    D. witness

15._____

16. Subpoenas may be issued without a court order by all of the following EXCEPT
    A. the clerk of the court or a judge where there is no clerk
    B. the attorney general, an attorney of record for a party to an action
    C. an arbitrator, a referee, or any member of a board, commission or committee authorized by law to hear
    D. a witness

16._____

17. A person for whose benefit an undertaking has been given to a _____ of the state may move, on notice to persons interested in the disposition of the proceeds, for leave to bring an action in his own name for breach of a condition.
    A. public officer, board or municipal corporation
    B. teacher, board, or municipal corporation
    C. CEO, teacher, or board
    D. accountant, teacher or board

17._____

18. A subpoenaed person who fails to comply with a court-ordered subpoena shall be liable to the person on whose behalf the subpoena was issued for a penalty not exceeding _____ and damages sustained by reason of the failure to comply.
    A. $50
    B. $100
    C. $150
    D. $200

18._____

19. A subpoenaed person who fails to comply with a subpoena not returnable in court shall be liable to the person on whose behalf the subpoena was issued for a penalty not exceeding _____ and damages sustained by reason of the failure to comply.
    A. $50
    B. $100
    C. $150
    D. $200

19._____

20. A _____ is a statement under oath that the pleading is true to the knowledge of the deponent, except to matters alleged on information and belief, and that as to those matters he believes to be true.
    A. verification
    B. pleading
    C. notification
    D. none of the above

20._____

21. The plaintiff may seek a default judgment against the defendant when
    A. the defendant failed to appear
    B. the defendant pleads or proceeds to trial of an action reached and called for trial
    C. the court orders a dismissal for any other neglect to proceed
    D. all of the above

21._____

22. If the plaintiff's claim is for a sum certain or for a sum which can by computation be made certain, application may be made to the clerk within _____ after a default.
    A. 6 months   B. 1 year   C. 2 years   D. 3 years

23. Except in a matrimonial action, at any time not later than _____ days before trial, any party against whom a claim is asserted, and against whom a separate judgment may be taken, may serve upon the claimant a written offer to allow judgment to be taken against him for a sum or property or to the effect therein specified, which costs then accrued.
    A. 5   B. 10   C. 15   D. 30

24. In every dental, podiatric or medical malpractice action, the court shall hold a mandatory settlement conference within _____ days after the filing of the note of issue and certificate or readiness or, if a party moves to vacate the note of issue and certificate of readiness, within _____ days after the denial of such motion.
    A. forty-five; forty-five
    B. forty-five; thirty
    C. thirty; thirty
    D. thirty; forty-five

25. A jury shall be composed of _____ persons.
    A. six   B. nine   C. ten   D. twelve

KEY (CORRECT ANSWERS)

1. D		11. D	
2. C		12. C	
3. C		13. B	
4. B		14. B	
5. D		15. D	
6. A		16. D	
7. D		17. A	
8. A		18. C	
9. D		19. A	
10. C		20. A	

21. D
22. B
23. B
24. A
25. A

EXAMINATION SECTION
TEST 1

DIRECTIONS: Each question or incomplete statement is followed by several suggested answers or completions. Select the one that BEST answers the question or completes the statement. *PRINT THE LETTER OF THE CORRECT ANSWER IN THE SPACE AT THE RIGHT.*

1. Which of the following is NOT a prerequisite to filing a class action lawsuit?
   A. The class is so numerous that joinder of all members is impracticable.
   B. All members of the class are approximately the same age, gender, or ethnicity.
   C. The claims or defenses of the representative parties are typical of the claims or defenses of the class.
   D. The representative parties will fairly and adequately protect the interests of the class.

   1.____

2. After the filing of a class action, may the court limit or otherwise exclude members of the class?
   A. Yes, the court may limit the class to those members who do not request exclusion within a specified time after notice.
   B. Yes, if the class appeals to exclude certain members of the action
   C. No, under no circumstances may the court exclude members of the class
   D. No,, however if one of the class members dies he or she may be excluded by default

   2.____

3. Jason prevailed on his motion to proceed in his lawsuit as a poor person. Jason also prevails in his lawsuit.
   Does Jason have to pay any of the court costs or fees, such as filing fees?
   A. No, because he prevailed on his motion to proceed as a poor person
   B. No, but he can choose to pay court costs and fees now that he has prevailed in his lawsuit
   C. Yes, the court may direct him to pay all or part of the costs and fees out of his recovery
   D. Yes he must revert all of his recovery over to the court

   3.____

4. When Liz started her job as a stockbroker, she signed an employment contract which, in part, stated that all employment related disputes would be heard in Orange County, New York. Liz lives in Albany and her employer is based in Nassau County. Liz has since quit her job and sued her former employer. Where will Liz's trial MOST likely take place?
   A. Orange County   B. Nassau County
   C. Albany County   D. Kings County

   4.____

5. The proper or most convenient location for trial of a case is also known as
   A. res ipsa   B. jurisdiction   C. venue   D. locale

   5.____

6. When a defendant has failed to appear, plead or proceed to trial of an action reached and called for trial, the plaintiff may seek a(n) _____ against him or her.
   A. detainee judgment
   B. indictment
   C. default judgment
   D. restitution

6.____

7. Kevin borrowed money from Rich and alleges that the contract he signed with the repayment terms—which Rich drafted—was materially altered after Kevin signed it.
Instead of a complaint, Kevin may serve Rich with notice of motion for _____ supporting papers along with a summons.
   A. summary judgment and
   B. default judgment and
   C. subpoena and record with
   D. a complaint with

7.____

8. Under what conditions may a temporary restraining order be granted without notice?
The plaintiff must show that
   A. immediate and irreparable injury, loss or damages will result
   B. harm is likely to occur if a temporary restraining order is not granted
   C. a likelihood of death is more probable than not if a temporary restraining order is not granted
   D. injury to personal or real property is a certainty if a temporary restraining order is not granted

8.____

9. Michelle lives in Connecticut. She was served with a subpoena to appear for an examination before trial in New York.
Is Michelle entitled to money for her attendance at the examination before trial?
   A. No, because she was served with a subpoena
   B. No, unless the examination before trial exceeds three hours in duration
   C. No, unless the examination before trial exceeds six hours in duration
   D. Yes

9.____

10. A judgment which declares the rights of the parties without ordering anything be done by either party is also known as a
    A. summons
    B. declaratory judgment
    C. default judgment
    D. summary judgment

10.____

11. What must be included in every complaint, counterclaim, cross-claim, interpleader complaint, and third party complaint?
    A. Demand for relief
    B. Monetary relief
    C. Answer
    D. Address of the respondent

11.____

12. In a wrongful death suit, the complaint must contain a _____ but shall not contain _____.
    A. prayer for relief; the amount of damages sought
    B. demand for answers; the amount of punitive damages sought
    C. name of the deceased; the amount of nominal damages recovered
    D. name of the deceased; the amount of damages sought

12.____

13. Suzanne wants to sue her dentist for malpractice.
    What document must accompany her complaint that is unique to medical, dental, and podiatric malpractice actions?
    A. Subpoena for the dental office's assistant
    B. Certificate of merit
    C. Certificate of summons
    D. A demand for specific relief

14. Assume the same facts as Question 13.
    Who must prepare the document identified in the above question?
    A. Attorney for the plaintiff
    B. Court clerk where the action is filed
    C. The plaintiff
    D. The respondent's attorney

15. In response to a complaint filed by her insurance company against her, Amy wants to respond to each allegation separately.
    Which of the following is NOT a proper response to each allegation or statement in the complaint?
    A. Deny the statements known or believed to be untrue
    B. Assert certain statements may be true
    C. Specify which statements Amy does not have knowledge or information sufficient to form a belief
    D. Admit to the allegations

16. The Latin term "res ipsa loquitor" is applicable in which of the following circumstances?
    A. A pre-meditated homicide
    B. An accident where negligence is inferred
    C. A petty larceny that is committed by two or more conspiring minors
    D. A robbery that occurs during a felony trespass

17. Statements in a pleading are required to be asserted with
    A. certainty   B. honesty   C. specificity   D. particularity

18. When is an index number assigned?
    A. The filing of a summons and complaint
    B. Summons with notice or petition
    C. When the proceeding is commenced in supreme or county court
    D. All of the above

19. If personal service is completed by mail, how must the service be mailed?
    A. Priority mail   B. Regular mail
    C. First class mail   D. E-mail

20. Which of the following is a ground for removal?
    A. By supreme court for mistake in choice of court
    B. From court of limited jurisdiction
    C. On consent to court of limited jurisdiction
    D. All of the above

21. Can personal service be completed upon an infant?
    A. No
    B. No, unless the child is emancipated
    C. No, unless the infant is old enough to sign the complaint and can attest they have been personally served
    D. Yes

22. A person whom the court has determined because of physical or mental limitation requires another individual to handle his or her affairs is known as a
    A. conservator   B. guardian
    C. guardian ad litem   D. conservatee

23. Mike and John both want to sue their former employer, Ace Enterprises. Mike alleges that he was discriminated against and fired because of his age. John alleges that he was discriminated against because of his religion and retaliated against for filing a complaint against his boss with Ace's Human Resource Department. After filing their complaint, the court decides that each claim should be litigated separately.
    The court will order a _____ of the claims.
    A. separation   B. severance   C. disjoinder   D. joinder

24. If triable issues of fact are raised in a dispute and the parties do not demand a jury trial to decide those issues, at what point is the right to a jury trial deemed waived?
    A. The start of the trial
    B. At the start of opening argument
    C. At the conclusion of closing arguments
    D. At appeal

25. An attorney of record may _____ or be changed by order of the court in which the action is pending, upon _____ on such notice.
    A. withdraw; notice   B. recant; motion
    C. recant; notice   D. withdraw; motion

KEY (CORRECT ANSWERS)

1. B
2. A
3. C
4. A
5. C

6. C
7. A
8. A
9. D
10. B

11. A
12. A
13. B
14. A
15. B

16. B
17. D
18. D
19. C
20. D

21. D
22. D
23. B
24. A
25. D

TEST 2

DIRECTIONS: Each question or incomplete statement is followed by several suggested answers or completions. Select the one that BEST answers the question or completes the statement. *PRINT THE LETTER OF THE CORRECT ANSWER IN THE SPACE AT THE RIGHT.*

1. Kim's attorney died in the middle of her trial. What is the legal result of her attorney's death?
   A. Kim will need to stand trial without representation.
   B. Kim's rights are unaltered by the death.
   C. Kim has five days to find another attorney or continue with the trial without representation.
   D. Kim has fourteen business days to find another attorney or continue with the trial without representation.

   1.____

2. How does a lawsuit typically commence?
   A. By the filing of a subpoena
   B. By the return of an indictment
   C. By the filing of a summons and complaint
   D. By acknowledgement of the wrongful act

   2.____

3. A court may exercise jurisdiction over a person, property, or
   A. chattel
   B. status
   C. remaindermen
   D. entitlement

   3.____

4. A&B Corporation is a Kentucky-based business that sells personal fans that have a "I love New York" logo on the product. The company only sells these products in the State of New York. One of the company's fans has caught fire and the purchasing customer, Michelle, wants to sue the company. Can a New York court exercise jurisdiction over A&B Corp.?
   A. Yes, because the company transacts business within the state
   B. No, because the company is based in Kentucky
   C. No, because the product was not intended to hurt anyone
   D. No, because the company has not availed themselves of New York jurisdiction

   4.____

5. A person who owes a debt to a judgment debtor, or a person other than the judgment debtor who has property in his possession or custody in which a judgment debtor has an interest is known as a
   A. lien holder   B. garnishee   C. beneficiary   D. debtor

   5.____

6. Which of the following qualifies as "real property"?
   A. Daniel's home in Nassau County
   B. Kim's jewelry gifted from her mother
   C. Tom's car which he purchased using credit
   D. Tanya's bank account, worth $5,600

   6.____

7. A complaint and answer are known as
   A. pleadings   B. responses   C. demands   D. interrogatories

8. The individual or individuals who replace a juror who has died, become ill or otherwise cannot serve are known as _____ jurors.
   A. replacement   B. rescinded   C. alternate   D. substitute

9. A trial without a jury is also known as a _____ trial.
   A. de novo   B. bench   C. demand   D. benchmarked

10. Every court in which a special proceeding to enforce a money judgment may be commenced shall have power to punish a contempt of _____ committed with respect to an enforcement procedure.
    A. court   B. issue   C. punishment   D. authority

11. According to Civil Practice Laws and Rules, the interest rate is _____ per annum.
    A. 4%   B. 5%   C. 6%   D. 9%

12. Jake and Sam have settled their contract dispute after months of discovery. As the settling defendant, how many days does Sam have to pay Jake?
    A. Ten   B. Twenty-one   C. Thirty   D. Ninety

13. Assume the same facts as in Question 12, except assume that Sam never paid Jake after the settlement.
    What legal recourse can Jake pursue against Sam?
    Jake may
    A. enter a judgment against Sam and demand interest from the date the stipulation discounting action were tendered
    B. enter a summary judgment against Sam
    C. enter a discourse judgment against Sam
    D. return an indictment against Sam

14. What is the difference between cross-claims versus a counterclaim?
    A. A counterclaim is a claim against an individual who may be involved in the claims at issue.
    B. A cross-claim is a claim against one or more individuals who may be involved in the claims at issue.
    C. A counterclaim is a direct claim against the person who initiated the lawsuit, whereas a cross-claim is a suit against a co-defendant or co-plaintiff.
    D. A counterclaim and cross-claim are interchangeable terms.

15. Personal service upon a court consisting of three or more judges may be made by
    A. delivering the summons to the court clerk's office
    B. e-mailing any one of the judges
    C. delivering the summons to any one of them
    D. delivering the summons to any one of the judge's clerk(s)

16. If an action does not have a limitation specifically prescribed by law then the limitation to commence an action is _____ years.
    A. five   B. six   C. eight   D. ten

17. Which of the following actions have a limitation of six years to commence?
    A. An action upon a sealed instrument
    B. An action based upon mistake
    C. An action based on fraud
    D. All of the above

18. Which of the following actions must be commenced within ten years?
    A. To redeem from a mortgage
    B. An action based on fraud
    C. An action upon a sealed instrument
    D. An action based on mistake

19. Can civil and criminal actions be merged together?
    A. Yes, if the actions concern the same individual
    B. Yes, but the civil action must be heard before the criminal action can commence
    C. Yes, but the criminal action must be heard before the civil action can commence
    D. No

20. If a party dies and the claim for or against him is not thereby extinguished, the court shall order substitution of the proper parties.
    An example of a substitute party is
    A. the estate of the deceased
    B. the sibling of the deceased
    C. the spouse of the deceased
    D. any of the above are possible substituted parties

21. Kate casually dated a man who introduced himself as Danny. After seeing one another for two weeks, Danny stole all of Kate's credit cards and began to open up credit cards in her name without her authorization. Kate never discovered Danny's last name.
    If Kate does not know the name or the identity of someone who should be named as a party in her lawsuit, may she commence the suit?
    A. Yes, as the filings can be amended accordingly
    B. No because she must know Danny's last name to commence a suit against him
    C. No, because Kate should have known that Danny would steal from her
    D. No, unless Danny can be located and prove his legal name in a sworn and written statement

22. A defendant's or lawyer's objection to a proposed juror, made without needing to give a reason, is also known as a
    A. peremptory challenge   B. juror challenge
    C. stare decisis   D. en banc challenge

23. Must a jury be unanimous to return a decision in a trial? 23.____
    A. Yes, a jury must be unanimous
    B. Yes, unless an alternate juror is substituted for a juror that died during the trial
    C. No, unless an alternate juror is substituted for a juror that died during the trial
    D. No

24. Michelle is a potential juror in a shareholder derivative suit. Ed is suing 24.____
    the Bank of Apple, a public company. Michelle holds stock in the Bank of
    Apple and discloses this fact in the voir dire process.
    What is the likely outcome of Michelle's disclosure?
    Michelle will
    A. be dismissed as a potential juror for cause
    B. be chosen as an alternate juror
    C. likely be chosen as a juror despite her disclosure
    D. likely be questioned by the judge and identified as a bias juror

25. At the close of the evidence in a trial, either the plaintiff or the defense may 25.____
    file a written request to the judge that the court instruct the jury on _____ as set
    forth in the respective written requests.
    A. the law
    B. the facts
    C. the weight that should be applied to the evidence
    D. none of the above

KEY (CORRECT ANSWERS)

1. B
2. C
3. B
4. A
5. B

6. A
7. A
8. C
9. B
10. A

11. D
12. B
13. A
14. C
15. C

16. B
17. D
18. A
19. D
20. D

21. A
22. A
23. D
24. A
25. A

EXAMINATION SECTION
TEST 1

DIRECTIONS: Each question or incomplete statement is followed by several suggested answers or completions. Select the one that BEST answers the question or completes the statement. *PRINT THE LETTER OF THE CORRECT ANSWER IN THE SPACE AT THE RIGHT.*

1. Peter Poe has been arrested on a charge of petit larceny. A search of police files indicates prior convictions for possessing a dangerous weapon and for illegally using the same. According to Criminal Procedure Law, it would be correct to state, with respect to the release of Poe on bail when arraigned in the court indicated, that he 1.____

    A. can be released on bail by a judge of the district court because such judges can admit to bail perpetrators of any crime
    B. can be released on bail by a judge of the criminal court of the City of New York because petit larceny is a misdemeanor
    C. cannot be released on bail by a judge of the criminal court of the City of New York because Poe has had two prior convictions
    D. cannot be released on bail by a judge of the district court because such judges can only admit to bail defendants charged with an offense

2. John Doe has been arrested in New York County charged therein with murder, first degree. According to Criminal Procedure Law, it would be correct to state, with respect to the release of Doe on bail, that he 2.____

    A. can be released on bail by a justice of the Supreme Court of New York State
    B. can be released on bail by a justice of the Court of Special Sessions of the City of New York
    C. cannot be released on bail by anyone if he had ever before attempted to commit a felony
    D. cannot be released on bail under any circumstances, except by a judge of the district court

3. John Doe has been arrested by an officer on patrol at night and brought to the station house for booking on a charge of disorderly conduct under Section 722 of the Penal Law. According to Criminal Procedure Law, the desk officer must release Doe on bail for appearance before a magistrate the next morning if Doe was charged with 3.____

    A. interfering with a person by placing his hand near such person's pocketbook or pocket
    B. soliciting men for lewd purposes in a public place
    C. engaging in an illegal occupation
    D. causing a disturbance in a bus or acting in a manner disturbing or offensive to others

4. John Doe has been arrested on a charge of disorderly conduct under Section 722 of the Penal Law. The one of the following offenses covered by this section for which Criminal Procedure Law requires the court's approval prior to admitting him to bail is 4.____

    A. jostling against or unnecessarily crowding a person in a public place
    B. acting in such a manner as to interfere with others

C. congregating on a public street and refusing to move on when ordered by the police
D. shouting outside a building at night to the annoyance of a considerable number of persons

5. The hours during which a police officer of superior rank must take bail for a misdemeanor are limited by Criminal Procedure Law to the hours between

   A. 11 A.M. and 8 A.M. the next morning
   B. 2 P.M. and 8 A.M. the next morning
   C. 11 A.M. and 2 P.M. the same day
   D. 2 P.M. and 11 A.M. the next morning

6. Billy Doe, a 13-year-old boy, is the only witness to a crime committed by his 22-year-old uncle with whom he has been staying while on a visit to New York City. According to Criminal Procedure Law, with respect to the production of the child in court, it would be correct to state that a

   A. personal recognizance in writing shall be accepted from Billy's parent or guardian only
   B. separate personal recognizance must be taken by the court for each production of the child pending the final termination of the proceedings
   C. personal recognizance shall not be accepted in this case from any person
   D. personal recognizance shall be vacated on failure to produce Billy in court as ordered and Billy himself taken into custody thereafter

7. The one of the following prerequisites for a permit to possess or dispose of firearms anywhere in this state, according to Penal Law is that the applicant must

   A. file a separate new application for each weapon if he wishes at any time to amend his license to include one or more weapons, if he is licensed either to possess weapons as an individual or as a dealer
   B. be a resident of the county in which the weapon is to be used, if he is applying for a license to possess and carry a weapon as a merchant or employee of a financial institution
   C. not have been convicted of either a misdemeanor or a felony, if he is applying for a permit to possess and carry concealable firearms
   D. be a citizen of the United States and over 21 years of age, if he wishes to be either a gunsmith or a dealer in firearms

8. John Doe, a barber, who has been posing as a surgeon specializing in abortions, is on trial. He is charged with having performed an illegal abortion which resulted in the death of Jane X. Before she died, Jane X made a dying declaration naming Doe as the person who had performed the illegal operation. According to Criminal Procedure Law, it would be correct to state that in this prosecution of Doe for abortion Jane X's dying declaration shall

   A. be admitted in evidence without any restrictions
   B. be admitted in evidence subject to the same restrictions as in cases of homicide
   C. not be admitted in evidence
   D. not be admitted in evidence if Jane X voluntarily submitted to the operation fully aware of its possible consequences

9. John Doe, the defendant on a robbery charge, has been released on bail in Manhattan. He goes to the farm home of his parents in Ulster County and fails to appear in court as ordered. As a result, his bail is forfeited and a bench warrant is issued in New York County for his arrest. Criminal Procedure Law provides, with respect to the service of such a bench warrant, that it may

   A. not be served outside New York County, the county of issue
   B. be served in Ulster County, but only after being endorsed by a magistrate of that county
   C. be served in Ulster County without being endorsed by a magistrate of that county
   D. be served in any county, in the same manner as a warrant of arrest, without any exceptions

10. John Smith, an accountant for the Alden Corporation, is dismissed after 20 years with the organization. Angry and disgruntled with the treatment accorded to him by the company, Smith tells Bill Jones, a neighbor, about all he had done to build up the company. He tells Jones how *cheap* the company is and how easy it would be to rob it on any pay day because of the lack of protective devices. He says he hopes someone will do it some day, and goes into great detail about how it could be done successfully. About six months later, without any knowledge on Smith's part, Jones and his brothers, Jim and Bob, successfully rob the Alden Corporation treasurer as he is about to pay off the staff. The holdup nets $40,000.
    Four years later, Bob Jones is apprehended. He involves his brothers. Bill Jones, on questioning, describes how Smith had given him the idea for the crime.
    According to the Penal Law, it would be most correct to state that Smith

    A. cannot be charged with having any connection with the crime because it took place entirely without his knowledge
    B. can no longer be arrested or charged with any crime because the statute of limitations for robbery is four years
    C. can be arrested and charged only with being an accessory because he took no part in the actual commission of the crime
    D. can be arrested and charged with being a principal to the robbery

11. Charging his pretty wife with infidelity, Joe Doakes has slashed at her face with a razor, causing severe mutilation around her eyes, mouth, and cheeks. This action results in permanent ugly scars. He is taken into custody and held for trial on a charge of maiming. In order to sustain this charge, it is necessary that intent be shown. According to the Penal Law, in connection with intent, with respect to this crime, it is most correct to state that the

    A. disfigurement need not even have been inflicted with felonious intent
    B. injury must seriously diminish the victim's physical vigor
    C. disfigurement must be incapable of being repaired by plastic surgery
    D. mere infliction of the injury is presumptive evidence of the intent

12. Arthur Mason has been released on $50,000 bail as the alleged armed-robber of a supermarket. He fails to appear in court as ordered. According to the Penal Law, it would be most correct for the police to charge Mason, in addition to the original charge, with a

    A. felony for jumping bail, if he fails to surrender himself within 30 days
    B. misdemeanor for jumping bail, if he fails to surrender himself within 30 days

C. felony for jumping bail, if he fails to surrender himself within 15 days
D. misdemeanor for jumping bail, plus the loss of the $50,000 if he fails to surrender himself within 15 days

13. Bill Walters, who has been subpoenaed as a witness to a holdup murder, is approached by two men, who offer him $10,000 to testify falsely as to what he had seen. When he refuses, they threaten his life. He then agrees, but notifies the police as soon as the two men leave.
According to the Penal Law, the two men can be charged with

A. subornation of perjury
B. perjury
C. suppressing evidence
D. dissuading witness from testifying

14. According to the Penal Law with regard to the use of force or fear in the crime of robbery, it would be most correct to state that, to constitute robbery,

A. force may have been used to obtain possession of the property, but, if this did not occur, force must have been used to escape
B. the mere snatching of the property from the hand of the victim without his resistance and without force or violence by the offender is sufficient
C. fear is a necessary ingredient regardless of the value of the property taken
D. when there is nothing to inspire fear, superior force must have been used, and the property relinquished upon a struggle and upon compulsion

15. The State Legislature amended the section of the Penal Law dealing with the making of malicious telephone calls. The amendment added a provision which made it a misdemeanor for a person to maliciously use the telephone

A. to threaten to commit a crime against the person called
B. to threaten to commit a crime against the teenage daughter of the person called
C. for the purpose of using obscene language to any person of the female sex
D. for the purpose of using obscene language to a male child under the age of 16 years

16. Jane Doe, a model, posed in the nude for several lewd photographs. Joe Hoe did the actual photographing and developed 100 prints of each pose. John Coe, the distributor, was apprehended with all the prints in his possession except for the 10 copies of one pose which he had just sold to Peter Poe. Poe was apprehended at the same time with the purchased pictures in his hand. Under Section 1141 of the Penal Law (obscene prints and articles), it would be most proper to charge a violation thereof to

A. J. Doe and J. Hoe only
B. J. Coe and P. Poe only
C. all four persons
D. J. Doe, J. Hoe, and J. Coe only

17. According to the Penal Law, the one of the following who could be charged with the misdemeanor of violating the provisions governing immoral shows and exhibitions is

    A. an actor participating in the performance
    B. the manager of the theater or place who permits the immoral show though without knowledge of the type of performance involved
    C. the advertising manager of the show
    D. the owner of the premises who rented the theater to the producers of the show though without any knowledge of the type of performance involved

18. Two officers on radio motor patrol notice four men acting suspiciously in a parked automobile near a large jewelry store. Upon questioning, the officers learn that the car and its driver had been hired for the night by the other three men. Dissatisfied with the evasiveness of the three men with respect to their answers to some of the questions, the officers frisk all four. An unlicensed .45 automatic is found on one of the passengers who states it does not belong to him. The other passengers know nothing of the presence of the gun. According to the Penal Law, the presence of the gun is presumptive evidence of its possession by

    A. all the occupants of the automobile
    B. the individual possessing it only
    C. all the occupants except the driver
    D. the individual possessing it and also the real owner

19. John Doe, who has just been convicted of a felony, is being transferred from the city prison to the state prison at Dannemora. While he is waiting under guard at Grand Central Station, his brothers, James and William, try to overpower the guards in order to help John escape. They succeed but all three are apprehended in the western part of the state two weeks later. According to the Penal Law, James and William

    A. can be charged with a misdemeanor, which is next lesser in degree than the felony for which John was convicted
    B. can be charged with a felony because John was convicted of a felony
    C. cannot be charged with a felony, because no weapons were used and the guards were not injured
    D. can be charged with either a misdemeanor or a felony, depending on who originated the conspiracy

20. Roy Brown enters a drugstore and forces the proprietor into the back room at knife point. He takes all the money he finds in the cash register and in the pharmacist's pocket. He ties the pharmacist's hands behind his back with adhesive tape and puts tape across his mouth. He sees the pharmacist's 15-year-old daughter in the back room, tapes her hands and mouth, and carnally abuses the girl with the intention of eventually raping her. Before he can rape her, he is surprised by an officer who comes into the store to check whether anyone had come in for treatment of a stab wound. The would-be rapist is apprehended while in the act of carnally abusing the girl.
    According to the Penal Law, Brown, if convicted,

    A. cannot be considered within the province of the law dealing with sexual abuse unless he administered or forced the girl to take a poison or narcotic intended to weaken her resistance
    B. may be sentenced for each crime separately, but the sentences must run consecutively

C. must be given a definite sentence for armed robbery and also an indeterminate sentence for the sex offense
D. may, in place of the penalty for armed robbery, receive an indefinite sentence of one day to life for the sexual abuse

KEY (CORRECT ANSWERS)

1.	B	11.	D
2.	A	12.	A
3.	D	13.	C
4.	A	14.	D
5.	B	15.	D
6.	C	16.	C
7.	D	17.	C
8.	B	18.	B
9.	C	19.	B
10.	A	20.	D

EXAMINATION SECTION

TEST 1

DIRECTIONS: Each question or incomplete statement is followed by several suggested answers or completions. Select the one that BEST answers the question or completes the statement. *PRINT THE LETTER OF THE CORRECT ANSWER IN THE SPACE AT THE RIGHT.*

1. Which class of felonies are divided into subclasses?
   A. Class A B. Class B C. Class C D. Class D

2. Can a traffic infraction be classified as a misdemeanor?
   A. Yes, if the punishment is less than one year of imprisonment
   B. Yes, if the punishment is less than fifteen months of imprisonment
   C. No, unless specified in the judgment
   D. No

3. Bryan smuggles cocaine out of Mexico in his infant daughter's diaper. He and his daughter are caught de-boarding from a plane at John F. Kennedy Airport.
   At arraignment, Bryan will MOST likely be charged with a
   A. misdemeanor   B. traffic infraction
   C. traffic violation   D. drug trafficking felony

4. A "juvenile offender" is defined as a person _____ years old who is criminally responsible for an act constituting murder in the second degree or such conduct as a sexually motivated felony.
   A. twelve B. thirteen C. fourteen D. fifteen

5. The New York Penal Law defines "child day care provider" by the definition used in what other law?
   A. Child Welfare Act   B. Social Services Law
   C. Family Court Act   D. Surrogates Court Clerk Law

6. Pursuant to the New York Penal Law, a felony without specification of the classification is deemed a Class _____ felony.
   A. A B. B C. D D. E

7. The MAXIMUM penalty for a Class B felony is _____ thousand dollars.
   A. ten B. twenty C. thirty D. fifty

8. Tony was convicted of stealing a car, which carries a felony designation. Tony maintains that he simply wanted to go for a joyride, but the victim alleges that $4,000 was in the car when it was stolen. The car was eventually returned to the victim; however, the cash was never recovered.
   Can the court legally demand that Tony replay the cash that was never recovered?

A. Yes, because that is the amount gained from the commission of the crime
B. No, because one cannot prove he stole the cash
C. No, because Tony simply wanted a joyride
D. No, because the cash was not insured by the vehicle's owner

9. A sentence to pay a fine for a Class A misdemeanor shall not exceed _____ dollars or an amount equivalent to double the value of the property unlawfully disposed of in the commission of the crime.
   A. five hundred
   B. eight hundred
   C. one thousand
   D. two thousand

9._____

10. Marcel posted an advertisement on social media selling a new guitar. A buyer forwarded Marcel $500 and Marcel never delivered the product as he never had a guitar to sell. Marcel was later convicted of the misdemeanor of false advertising. The court imposes an alternative sentence for the crime.
    What is the MOST likely fine Marcel will need to pay?
    A. $250, half the amount he received from the crime
    B. $750, a 50% increase in the amount of money he received from the crime
    C. $1,000, double the amount of money he received from the crime
    D. Marcel will not have to pay any money as he was convicted of a misdemeanor

10._____

11. Which of the following are classified as Class A misdemeanors?
    A. Escape in the third degree
    B. Perjury in the third degree
    C. Identify theft in the third degree
    D. All of the above

11._____

12. Which of the following is a Class B misdemeanor?
    A. Reckless endangerment of property
    B. Coercion in the second degree
    C. Making graffiti
    D. Arson in the fifth degree

12._____

13. Tim is convicted of two misdemeanors, one which is classified as Class A and the other is classified as Class B. For the Class A misdemeanor, the court imposes a term of eight months imprisonment.
    Can the court impose a fine of $500 for the Class B misdemeanor?
    A. Yes, the court can impose a fine in addition to the term of imprisonment
    B. No, the court cannot impose a fine in excess of $250 as this is deemed excessive punishment and not available for appeal
    C. No, the court cannot impose a fine in excess of $400 as this is deemed excessive punishment and not available for appeal
    D. No, the court cannot impose a fine in addition to the term of imprisonment if the offenses were committed through a single act and one offense is a material element of the other

13._____

14. If ABC Corporation is convicted of a felony, what is the maximum amount the company will have to pay?
    A. Five thousand dollars
    B. Ten thousand dollars
    C. Fifteen thousand dollars
    D. An amount not to exceed double the amount of shareholders the company has on record as of the date of the commission of the crime

    14.____

15. Soliciting or providing support for an act of terrorism in the second degree is classified as a
    A. misdemeanor
    B. violation
    C. Class D felony
    D. felony of an unspecified degree

    15.____

16. Richie is convicted of making a terrorist threat. What is this offense classified as?
    A. Class D felony
    B. Unclassified felony
    C. Unclassified misdemeanor
    D. Civil offense

    16.____

17. A firearm that is actually shared, made available, sold, exchanged, given or disposed of among or between two or more persons, at least one of whom is not authorized pursuant to law possess such firearm is defined as a
    A. roundabout gun
    B. community gun
    C. shared gunner
    D. civil weapon

    17.____

18. Judge O'Neill is currently presiding over a murder trial, where the defendant ran over a young child with his car. The defense alleges the crime was an accident and that the defendant should be found guilty, if at all, of a lesser offense. The prosecution argues that the defendant intended to kill the victim. In chambers, Judge O'Neill explains to his law clerk that in order to find the defendant guilty of the more serious crime charged, he must have the culpable mental state during the commission of the crime.
    A culpable mental state means
    A. intentionally, knowingly or recklessly or with criminal negligence
    B. knowingly but not intentionally
    C. negligent intent but not knowingly or recklessly
    D. none of the above

    18.____

19. Derek wants to kill Al who works at the local gym. Al's twin brother exits the gym at 11:45 P.M. and Derek shoots him. Derek alleges that because he meant to kill Al and not Al's twin brother, he should not be found guilty of murder.
    What is the likely verdict?
    A. Not guilty, because of a mistake of fact
    B. Not guilty, because Derek has confessed to his crimes
    C. Guilty, because of a mistake of fact
    D. Guilty, because the crime of murder still occurred

    19.____

4 (#1)

20. Any article or thing which a person confined in a detention facility is prohibited from obtaining or possessing by statute, rule, regulation or order is known as
    A. illicit materials
    B. contraband
    C. magazines
    D. weaponry

20.____

21. Which of the following offenses relating to custody is classified as a misdemeanor?
    A. Escape in the third degree
    B. Absconding from temporary release in the second degree
    C. Resisting arrest
    D. All of the above

21.____

Questions 22-25.

DIRECTIONS: Questions 22 through 25 are to be answered on the basis of the following fact pattern.

Ralph was kidnapped at gunpoint outside of Syracuse. He was taken to an abandoned warehouse by his captors and kept for nearly three days without food or water. Ralph never saw the gun or any other weapons while he was in captivity, but was told he would be killed if he did not go to the bank and empty his bank accounts. After his captors dropped him off at a local bank, Ralph went inside and closed all of his accounts and left the cash outside of the bank in an envelope and ran. Later, Ralph was able to identify all of his captors and at trial alleged that he emptied his bank accounts in duress.

22. Under these circumstances, can Ralph allege that he was under duress?
    A. Yes, he can assert duress as an affirmative defense
    B. No, because Ralph never saw a weapon after the initial kidnapping
    C. No, because Ralph emptied his account on his own free will
    D. No, because Ralph does not know for sure if the captors ever received the cash

22.___-

23. When is duress NOT available as a defense?
    A. When a person intentionally or recklessly places himself in a situation in which it is probable that he will be subjected to duress
    B. Duress is always available as a defense
    C. Duress is a rarely used defense and is not available for adults who are capable of acting of their own free will
    D. Duress is not available as a defense if the defense of intentional negligence is also used

23.____

24. If Ralph's captors are convicted of a Class B violent felony, what is the MOST likely outcome of the sentencing in terms of imprisonment?
    A. 1-3 years   B. 5-10 years   C. 5-25 years   D. 25 years to life

24.____

25. Which of the following is MOST likely to be considered in the sentencing of Ralph's captors? 25.____
    A. Familial relationship to Ralph, if any
    B. The location Ralph was abducted and how far that location is from Ralph's primary residence or domiciliary
    C. Prior criminal history of each offender
    D. Ralph's age

KEY (CORRECT ANSWERS)

1.	A		11.	D
2.	D		12.	A
3.	D		13.	D
4.	B		14.	B
5.	B		15.	C
6.	D		16.	A
7.	C		17.	B
8.	A		18.	A
9.	C		19.	D
10.	C		20.	B

21.	D
22.	A
23.	A
24.	C
25.	C

TEST 2

DIRECTIONS: Each question or incomplete statement is followed by several suggested answers or completions. Select the one that BEST answers the question or completes the statement. *PRINT THE LETTER OF THE CORRECT ANSWER IN THE SPACE AT THE RIGHT.*

1. Prosecutors must prove that Abe and Luke's conspiracy derived from an intentional scheme to defraud investors.
   Which of the following is the MOST appropriate definition of scheme?
   A. A plan between two people to do an agreed upon activity
   B. Any plan, pattern device, contrivance, or course of action intended to deceive others
   C. A plan between three or more people to do something one of them is intent on finishing
   D. A topic of conversation shared between two or more people

   1.____

2. Corrupting the government in the fourth degree is classified as a Class ____ felony and requires that the individual committing the crime either be, or act in concert with a _____.
   A. E; public servant
   B. D; person of interest
   C. E; person of interest
   D. D; public servant

   2.____

3. A person commits the crime of _____ when being a public servant he or she commits a specified offense through the use of his or her public office.
   A. private coercion
   B. public corruption
   C. sentencing
   D. acting in dangerous concert

   3.____

4. Arson in the first degree and aggravated enterprise corruption are examples of
   A. A-1 felonies
   B. Class C felonies
   C. misdemeanors
   D. traffic violations

   4.____

5. If a felon sentence does not carry a term of imprisonment, which of the following will MOST likely be required of the defendant in lieu of jail?
   A. Parole
   B. Probation
   C. Active custody
   D. Recognizance

   5.____

6. Which of the following is a violation?
   A. Loitering
   B. Criminal solicitation in the second degree
   C. Welfare fraud in the third degree
   D. Bribing a labor official

   6.____

7. Maurice is found guilty of intentionally, and for no legitimate purpose, engaging in a course of conduct directed at his former co-worker, Michelle, that he knows is likely to cause reasonable fear of material harm. Maurice is convicted of which crime?
   A. Battery   B. Negligence   C. Stalking   D. Trespass

   7.____

8. Which of the following carries the LOWEST sanction and is not defined as a crime?
   A. Felony
   B. Misdemeanor
   C. Class A felony
   D. Violation

9. Which felony class is the MOST serious?
   A. Class B
   B. Class A
   C. Class E
   D. Class D

10. An "act" is considered the opposite of a(n) _____. As an example, during an interrogation into the disappearance of Andrew's cousin, Andrew fails to mention that he was the last person to see his cousin alive.
    A. response
    B. omission
    C. redaction
    D. impactful

11. A person acts _____ when his conscious objective is to cause such result or to engage in such conduct, whereas a person acts _____ when he is aware that his conduct is of such nature or that such circumstance exists.
    A. knowingly; recklessly
    B. knowingly; negligently
    C. knowingly; criminally
    D. intentionally; knowingly

12. Kristin was driving under the influence of alcohol when she crashed her brand new car into the front yard of Joe's house, killing his outdoor cat and knocking over his mailbox. Kristin argues that she is not liable for her actions because she was intoxicated at the time of the accident. Joe argues that Kristin intentionally crashed into his house.
    What is the effect of intoxication on liability?
    Evidence of intoxication
    A. may be offered whenever it is relevant to negate an element of the crime charged
    B. is always relevant in disputes involving a vehicle
    C. is only relevant if raised in the initial complaint or otherwise raised prior to opening arguments at trial
    D. never has any material effect on the defendant's liability

13. Any contest, game, gaming scheme or gaming device in which the outcome depends in a material degree upon an element of change is known as
    A. gambling
    B. illicit arson
    C. restriction to chance
    D. contest of chance

14. If the court imposes a fine for a felony, the court must also make a finding as to the _____ the crime.
    A. amount of the defendant's gain from
    B. defendant's age at the time of
    C. defendant's height at the time of
    D. financial liabilities of the defendant at the time of

15. Jeremy is convicted of a felony and required to pay $15,000 in fines, or double the amount of money he gained in the commission of his crime. The state comptroller is responsible for collecting moneys in excess of _____ received or collected in payment of a fine and depositing the same into the rehabilitative alcohol and substance treatment fund established by the state finance law.
In other words, the total sum of _____ will be deposited into the treatment fund.
    A. $5,000; $10,000
    B. $2,000; $13,000
    C. $14,000; $1,000
    D. $1,000; $14,000

16. Which of the following is MOST likely a condition of probation?
    A. Answer all reasonable inquiries by the probation officer
    B. Notify the probation officer prior to any change in address
    C. Notify the probation officer prior to any change in employment
    D. All of the above

17. When can a sentence requiring the defendant to submit to the use of an electronic monitoring device be imposed?
    A. Only where the court determines that such condition will advance public safety, probationer control or probationer surveillance
    B. Whenever the court pleases and for every type of offense involving a minor
    C. Electronic monitoring devices were deemed unlawful in the State of New York in 2005
    D. Only where the court determines that the defendant's family or alleged victim is in imminent danger

18. A condition of probation for a convicted sex offender, when the victim of the crime was under the age of eighteen, will always include a prohibition against which of the following?
Knowingly entering into
    A. or upon school grounds
    B. a movie theater
    C. or upon a library
    D. or upon a grocery store or other marketplace

19. Amara's trial begins on April 1, 2017 and lasts for three months. Amara is found guilty of the crime charged on June 1, 2017 but is not sentenced until September 15th. Amara is sentenced to probation on September 15, 2017 for a period of twelve months.
When does Amara's probation end?
    A. April 1, 2018
    B. June 1, 2018
    C. September 15, 2018
    D. August 1, 2018

20. A revocable sentence of imprisonment to be served on days or during certain periods of days, or both, specified by the court as part of the sentence is deemed a(n)
    A. conditional release
    B. unconditional sentence
    C. intermittent imprisonment
    D. restless release

21. A conviction of a violation shall be punishable by a fine not to exceed   21.____
    A. $250   B. $500   C. $1,000   D. $5,000

Questions 22-25.

DIRECTIONS: Questions 22 through 25 are to be answered on the basis of the following fact pattern.

Tom and Hank are hanging out after school when Tom dares Hank to steal graffiti on the side of an apartment building. Tom and Hank are both eighteen and graduating from high school in the spring. Tom and Hank are both apprehended during the commission of the crime.

22. A person is guilty of _____ when, with intent that another person engage in   22.____
    conduct constituting a crime, he solicits, requests, commands, importunes, or
    otherwise attempts to cause such other person to engage in such conduct.
    This crime is a violation of
    A. criminal solicitation in the fifth degree
    B. criminal trespass
    C. criminal restitution in the first degree
    D. burglary with an accessory

23. Hank alleges that he did not know that making graffiti is a crime, because   23.____
    he sees graffiti in New York City all the time.
    Has Hank proffered an affirmative defense to the crime of making graffiti?
    A. Yes, he can commit a crime if he did not know what he was doing was
       criminal
    B. Yes, because he offered his defense prior to the start of the trial and in all
       honesty
    C. No, because he was caught in the commission of the crime with another
       person
    D. No, because now knowing he was committing a crime does not absolve
       him of liability

24. Tom insists that he also did know that making graffiti is a crime. Tom is also   24.____
    being charged with possession of graffiti instruments. Making graffiti is a Class
    _____ misdemeanor whereas possession of graffiti instruments is a Class
    _____ misdemeanor.
    A. B; C   B. C; D   C. A; B   D. E; D

25. Given that the crimes Tom is being charged with are misdemeanors, what is   25.____
    the MAXIMUM term of imprisonment Tom is facing (in months)?
    A. Six   B. Twelve   C. Eighteen   D. Twenty-four

KEY (CORRECT ANSWERS)

1.	B	11.	D
2.	A	12.	A
3.	B	13.	D
4.	A	14.	A
5.	B	15.	A
6.	A	16.	D
7.	C	17.	A
8.	D	18.	A
9.	B	19.	D
10.	B	20.	C

21. C
22. A
23. D
24. C
25. B

EXAMINATION SECTION
TEST 1

DIRECTIONS: Each question or incomplete statement is followed by several suggested answers or completions. Select the one that BEST answers the question or completes the statement. *PRINT THE LETTER OF THE CORRECT ANSWER IN THE SPACE AT THE RIGHT.*

1. A _____ person is chargeable with the support of his or her spouse and, if possessed of sufficient means or able to earn such means, may be required to pay for his or her support a fair and reasonable sum, as the court may determine, having due regard to the circumstances of the respective parties. 1.____
    A. reasonable   B. married   C. sufficient   D. supportive

Questions 2-5.

DIRECTIONS: Questions 2 through 5 are to be answered on the basis of the following fact pattern.

Perry and Susan are married for five years. Their only child, Linda, is enrolled in a private elementary school when Perry and Susan divorce. Linda's school tuition is $12,000 per year. Perry currently earns $50,000 per year. As a real estate agent, Susan's salary fluctuates but on average she earns around $40,000 per year.

2. What is the combined parental income if Susan has full legal custody of Linda after the divorce? 2.____
    A. $50,000
    B. $40,000
    C. $90,000
    D. The sum cannot be determined if Susan's salary fluctuates

3. Perry recently lost his job and wants to have his child support modified. Can Perry request the support collection unit review the child support order for cost of living adjustment purposes? 3.____
    A. No, because Perry's job loss is not a result of a cost of living change
    B. Yes, because Perry lost his job
    C. Yes, but only if Perry can prove he has no income
    D. Yes, but only if Susan approves of the review

4. In the case of Perry, Susan, and Linda, the child support percentage is _____% of the combined parental income for one child. 4.____
    A. 17   B. 25   C. 29   D. 31

5. Perry earns extra money delivering newspapers on the weekends. He is paid by check by the distributor and earns cash tips around the holidays. Is this income he earns from his weekend job considered income for child support purposes?
    A. Only payment from the distributor is considered income.
    B. Only cash tips are considered income.
    C. Both checks and cash tips are considered income.
    D. Neither payment is considered income.

6. Where may proceedings to establish paternity be originated?
    A. In the county where the mother of the child lives
    B. In the county where the child resides or is found
    C. In the county where the putative father resides
    D. All of the above

7. Laila is eight months old and lives in Massachusetts with her mother. When Laila was two months old, Laila's mother decided to move out of New York State to flee from Laila's abusive father. Laila's mother would like to file a child support order.
   Where is Laila's home state?
    A. Massachusetts
    B. New York
    C. The state where the putative father resides
    D. The state of the most convenient venue

8. The term "issuing state" is defined as the state in which a tribunal issues a support order or renders a judgment determining
    A. parentage   B. jurisdiction   C. venue   D. domicile

9. James does not live in New York, but was staying in Albany with his mother when he was personally served with a summons and petition to enforce a child support order. James's son, Dex, lives in Brooklyn with James's ex-girlfriend.
   Can the New York Family Court exercise jurisdiction over James?
    A. No, because James does not live in New York
    B. No, because James does not live with Dex's mother
    C. Yes, because he was personally served within the state
    D. Yes, but only if James consents to jurisdiction

10. Which of the following parties are eligible to commence a family offense proceeding?
    A. The spouse of the respondent
    B. A duly authorized agency, association, or institution
    C. Any person on the court's motion
    D. All of the above

11. After the filing of a petition by the petitioner in a family offense proceeding, the court will
    A. issue a summons or issue a warrant
    B. advise all parties of the right to retain legal representation
    C. direct that the respondent post bail for the amount set by the court
    D. issue a commitment order directing the respondent be remanded to the custody of the county sheriff

11._____

12. A temporary order of protection is
    A. an admission of guilt
    B. proof of a crime
    C. not a finding of wrongdoing
    D. reason for probable issuance

12._____

Questions 12-15.

DIRECTIONS: Questions 12 through 15 are to be answered on the basis of the following fact pattern.

Bryan and his sister, Amanda, were involved in a physical altercation outside of their home in Buffalo, New York. Bryan is 25 and Amanda is 16. While it is unclear how the altercation began, the district attorney would like to investigate the incident further. After the hearing in Family Court, the district attorney requests a copy of the family offense proceeding.

13. May the Family Court provide a copy of the transcript to the district attorney?
    A. No, because the incident is not criminal in nature
    B. No, because family offense proceedings are sealed
    C. No, because family offense proceedings are not recorded or otherwise transcribed
    D. Yes

13._____

14. Where will the Family Court proceedings take place?
    A. In the county where the incident occurred
    B. In the county that Bryan chooses
    C. In the county that Amanda chooses
    D. In the county the district attorney chooses

14._____

15. Amanda has requested the court issue a TRO for her protection against her brother, Bryan. A TRO is also known as a
    A. temporary restitution order
    B. temporal restraining order
    C. temporary restraining order
    D. transitional restitution order

15._____

16. What information is contained in a permanency hearing report?
    A. The health and well-being of a child
    B. Reasonable efforts that have been made since the last hearing to promote permanency
    C. The recommended permanency plan for the child
    D. All of the above

16._____

17. Decisions and final orders of the Family Court are appealed to which judicial body?
    A. The appellate division of the Supreme Court of the Judicial Department in which the Family Court order was issued
    B. The surrogate's division of the Supreme Court of the Judicial Department in which the Family Court order was issued
    C. The Third Circuit Court
    D. The final appeals unit of the New York Supreme Court

17._____

18. An appeal as of right shall be taken by filing the _____ notice of appeal with the clerk of the Family Court in which the order was made and from which the appeal is taken. The appellant shall file _____ copies of such notice, together with the proof of service, with the clerk of the Family Court who shall forthwith transmit one copy of such notice to the clerk of the appropriate appellate division.
    A. first; three   B. original; two   C. first; three   D. original; four

18._____

19. Which court has exclusive original jurisdiction in proceedings to establish paternity?
    A. The Appellate Court   B. The Supreme Court
    C. The Family Court   D. Surrogates Court

19._____

20. Can Jeremy, who is 25, file a petition to return to foster care after being discharged from foster care?
    A. Yes, as he was previously in the foster care system
    B. Yes, as he is consenting to return to foster care of his own free will
    C. No, because he cannot return to foster care without the consent of his adoptive parents
    D. No, because he is 25

20._____

21. Judge O'Connor would like to visit the local elementary school to check in on two different students who were recently placed into foster care.
    May Judge O'Connor do so?
    A. Yes; the judge may do so in an official capacity
    B. Yes, but only if she does not identify herself as a judge
    C. Yes, but only if she does not identify herself as a public servant
    D. Yes, but only if she garners the consent of the foster care agency

21._____

22. What days may a warrant of arrest be executed?
    A. Monday through Friday   B. Weekends only
    C. Monday through Saturday   D. Any day of the week

22._____

23. At what time may a warrant of arrest be executed?
    A. Only between the hours of 9:00 A.M. and Midnight
    B. Only before 9:00 A.M.
    C. Only after sunset
    D. Any hour of the day or night

23._____

24. Shephard lives in Essex County, but sometimes stays with his mother who lives in Nassau County. Because of the distance between the two residences, Shephard has been spending increasingly more time with his mother and les time at his own residence in Essex County. While staying with his mother, Shephard is personally served with court papers relating to his paternity suit in Essex County.
Can the court exercise jurisdiction over Shephard in Nassau County?
    A. No, because Shephard is not a resident of Nassau County
    B. No, because Shephard did not waive his rights to be served in Nassau County
    C. Yes, because Shephard availed himself of the benefits of statewide travel
    D. Yes, because the Family Court may send proceeds in any matter in which it has jurisdiction into any county of the state for service or execution

24.____

25. Marie's son, Tom, is being accused of willful nonpayment of child support. Marie is furious with Tom's ex-wife and during the proceeding continues to berate and scream at Tom's attorney and the judge.
Can Marie be found guilty of contempt of court in Family Court?
    A. No, because contempt is reserved for criminal courts only
    B. No, because contempt is reserved for civil courts only
    C. Yes, because Marie is a danger to the parties' legal representation
    D. Yes

25.____

KEY (CORRECT ANSWERS)

1.	B		11.	A
2.	C		12.	C
3.	A		13.	D
4.	A		14.	A
5.	C		15.	D
6.	D		16.	D
7.	A		17.	A
8.	A		18.	B
9.	C		19.	C
10.	D		20.	D

21. A
22. D
23. D
24. D
25. D

TEST 2

DIRECTIONS: Each question or incomplete statement is followed by several suggested answers or completions. Select the one that BEST answers the question or completes the statement. *PRINT THE LETTER OF THE CORRECT ANSWER IN THE SPACE AT THE RIGHT.*

Questions 1-2.

DIRECTIONS: Questions 1 and 2 are to be answered on the basis of the following fact pattern.

Jim was recently made aware that his estranged wife, Marissa, has requested an order of protection from him.

1. What is the purpose of an order of protection? 1.____
   An order of protection is issued to
   A. compel the payment of child support
   B. stop violence within a family, or within an intimate relationship
   C. compel the payment of alimony or other support obligation
   D. warn the respondent that a restraining order will follow after the order of protection is stamped and filed

2. After Marissa requests the order of protection, what may Jim file in response? 2.____
   A. Jim is ineligible to file a response.
   B. Jim may file an answer to the petition and a counter-claim.
   C. Jim must file a summons to compel Marissa to provide evidence of abuse.
   D. Jim may file a demand for further discovery.

3. Teresa has commenced a proceeding in Family Court to prove the paternity of her daughter, Sara. Teresa has named Lewis as the respondent in her petition as she alleges he is Sara's father. After filing the paternity proceeding petition, the court may issue a summons which will require Lewis to do which of the following? 3.____
   A. Show cause why the declaration of paternity should not be made
   B. Respond to written discovery demands forwarded by Teresa and/or Teresa's legal counsel
   C. Appear in the Family Court in the county where Teresa currently resides to answer for the action
   D. Personally appear at a preliminary conference in the judge's chambers to respond to the petition

4. Which of the following is MOST likely to be linked to the issuance of a warrant by the Family Court? 4.____
   A. Proceeding to compel support by the mother
   B. Proceeding to compel support by the father
   C. A proceeding to challenge the testing directive
   D. All of the above

5. Which of the following are court rules that govern attorneys for children?
   A. Prescribed workload, including maximum number of children that can be represented at any given time
   B. The times that attorneys for children may enter and exit the courtroom for hearings
   C. The dates at which hearings can be scheduled, including which days of the week attorneys may appear for the hearings
   D. A requirement that all attorneys for children be a minimum age before engaging as counsel

6. Tina was placed on probation shortly after her proceeding to compel support for her daughter. As a condition of Tina's probation, she is ordered to abstain from drugs and alcohol. Tina has missed her last three appointments with her probation officer.
   According to the New York Family Court Act, if at any time during the period of probation the court has reasonable cause to believe that the respondent has violated a condition of the probation order, it may issue a _____ order.
   A. support   B. research   C. disciplinary   D. search

7. An order of sequestration may be issued for what purpose?
   Sequestration is the act of
   A. removing the respondent from the jurisdiction of the underlying hearing
   B. removing, separating, or seizing the possessions of the owner for the benefit of creditors
   C. holding possessions of the owner in trust for the benefit of the trust's beneficiaries
   D. compelling payment from a respondent who has absconded from custody

8. Upon a finding that a respondent has failed to comply with any lawful order of support, the court may do which of the following?
   A. Order the respondent to pay a money judgment
   B. Suspend the respondent's driving privileges
   C. The court may impose an order of sequestration upon the respondent
   D. All of the above

9. In New York City, which body represents the social services commissioner?
   A. Corporation Counsel of the City of New York
   B. The District Attorney's office
   C. Counsel of the Supreme Court of New York
   D. Counsel of the Appellate Division of the Supreme Court of New York

10. Stephanie and Danielle, each 10 years old, are half-sisters and live with their father. Stephanie was removed by Social Services and placed into foster care approximately one year ago. Danielle is being removed by Social Services. Where will Danielle MOST likely be placed?
    A. With Stephanie, as placement with half-siblings is presumptively in the best interests of the child
    B. With Stephanie, but only if Danielle so chooses

C. To a foster care that is separate from Stephanie so as to not confuse or alienate the child
D. To the Department of Social Services and Probation

11. A child under the age of eighteen who is in a state of want or suffering to a lack of sufficient food, clothing, shelter, or medical or surgical care is referred to as a(n)
    A. abandoned child
    B. child in need of supervision
    C. destitute child
    D. desperate child

12. The term "arrears" generally refers to
    A. past money owed or due
    B. the percentage of alimony in dispute
    C. the amount of child support in dispute
    D. a fixed amount of money due to the court (i.e, escrow)

13. A destitute child proceeding may be originated by which person or party?
    A. The Commissioner of Social Services only
    B. An authorized child services agency
    C. The parents of the child
    D. Any caretaker of the child

14. A minor who is the subject of a _____ or a person in need of supervision proceedings is presumed to lack the requisite knowledge and maturity to waive the appointment of an attorney.
    A. child support proceeding
    B. family offense proceeding
    C. juvenile delinquency
    D. child placement hearing

15. The costs for attorneys for children shall be payable by the
    A. Commissioner of Social Services
    B. Family Court in which the attorney serves
    C. State of New York
    D. City of New York

16. A proceeding to determine capacity is MOST likely to occur in which of the following scenarios?
    A. Gabriel, 16, committed a misdemeanor while playing a game of "truth or dare" with his three closest friends
    B. Anne, 15, a mentally distributed teenager who sexually assaulted her younger brother
    C. Rachel, 21, who has a violent streak and often yells and hits her parents
    D. Jamal, 20, who recently stole a bike from a neighbor's backyard

17. The court shall not consent to the entry of an admission unless it has advised the respondent of his or her right to a
    A. fact-finding hearing
    B. trial by jury
    C. trial by the bench
    D. pre-trial conference

4 (#2)

18. Jamie's attorney would like to file a motion to seal after a finding of delinquency on Jamie's behalf. The notice of such motion shall be served upon the presentment agency not less than _____ days prior to the return date of the motion. Answering affidavits shall be served at least _____ days before such time.
    A. 10; 5   B. 8; 2   C. 11; 6   D. 15; 9

19. Daniel is an attorney for a large law firm in Manhattan. Daniel and his wife are in the midst of a divorce and related child support hearing. The court has asked Daniel's employer to provide full information with respect to Daniel's earnings.
    Must Daniel's employer comply?
    A. No, because the information is not necessary in the child support hearing
    B. No, unless Daniel consents to the release of such information
    C. No, because the court is not authorized to retrieve such information
    D. Yes

20. Does an indigent adult have the right to be represented by counsel and/or to confer with counsel?
    An indigent
    A. adult may only confer with counsel, but must pay for the legal representation
    B. adult may be represented by counsel upon the consent of the court
    C. adult may be represented by counsel but cannot choose his or her counsel
    D. person has the right to be represented by counsel of his or her choosing

21. The parents of Matilda would like to stop her placement into foster care. Matilda's parents terminated their parental rights nearly three years, but heard that Matilda would be placed into foster care by her adoptive parents.
    Which party is the MOST appropriate person(s) to file a motion to terminate Matilda's placement into foster care?
    A. Matilda   B. Matilda's birth parents
    C. Matilda's adoptive parents   D. Matilda's attorney

22. Which of the following qualifies as an initial appearance?
    A. The preliminary conference between the parties' legal representation
    B. The date the respondent first appears before the court after the petition is filed
    C. The first day of a trial in which the respondent and petitioner will see one another
    D. The judge's first order

23. Nontestimonial evidence from the respondent, which may be ordered by the court upon motion made by the petitioner, is also known as
    A. a subpoena-related inquiry   B. discovery
    C. interrogation   D. a demand by investigation

24. If a motion under the motion to terminate placement is denied, it may not be renewed for a period of _____ days after the denial, unless the order of denial permits renewal at an earlier time.
    A. 30   B. 60   C. 90   D. 120

25. A motion that is renewed and filed after the required period of time is also referred to as a(n) _____ motion.
    A. recurring   B. successive   C. unrestricted   D. untimed

KEY (CORRECT ANSWERS)

1.	B		11.	C
2.	B		12.	A
3.	A		13.	A
4.	D		14.	C
5.	A		15.	C
6.	D		16.	B
7.	B		17.	A
8.	D		18.	B
9.	A		19.	D
10.	A		20.	D

21.	C
22.	B
23.	B
24.	C
25.	B

EXAMINATION SECTION

TEST 1

DIRECTIONS: Each question or incomplete statement is followed by several suggested answers or completions. Select the one that BEST answers the question or completes the statement. *PRINT THE LETTER OF THE CORRECT ANSWER IN THE SPACE AT THE RIGHT.*

1. Gary owns an apartment in downtown Brooklyn. Gary resides in Watkins Glen and rents the apartment in Brooklyn. His tenant moved out of the Brooklyn apartment about two weeks ago. Since then, he has received e-mails from friends in Brooklyn that a transient individual, Sean, has been sleeping in the apartment by breaking in the back window.
   Does a landlord-tenant relationship exist between Gary and Sean?
   A. Yes, because Gary owns the apartment
   B. Yes, because Sean is the rightful tenant of the apartment
   C. No, because Sean has not been in possession of the apartment for thirty consecutive days
   D. No, because Sean has not informed Gary that he wants to be Gary's tenant

1.____

2. If a landlord/tenant relationship exists and the grounds are met for a special proceeding to take place, the landlord must give the tenant _____ day notice of the special proceeding.
   A. ten   B. fifteen   C. twenty   D. twenty-five

2.____

3. A real property proceedings may be brought by which of the following party(ies)?
   A. A landlord
   B. A person forcibly put or kept out
   C. The lessee of the premises, entitled to possession
   D. All of the above

3.____

4. A special proceeding to recover real property can be initiated in which of the following venues?
   A. County court
   B. District court
   C. Justice court
   D. Each of the above, and a court of civil jurisdiction in a city

4.____

5. How does James start a special proceeding to recover real property from his tenant, Marisol?
   A. James should file a complaint in civil court.
   B. James should file a notice of petition and petition to commence the action.
   C. James must arrange for the service of a subpoena upon Marisol.
   D. James should attempt to evict Marisol himself once Marisol stops paying rent.

5.____

Questions 6-8.

DIRECTIONS: Questions 6 through 8 are to be answered on the basis of the following fact pattern.

Jeremy wants to buy property in an up-and-coming neighborhood of Suffolk County. He enlists his friend and former co-worker, Danielle, to help him find a suitable house at a bargain. Danielle is a native of the area in which Jeremy wants to buy. Jeremy buys a home and asks Danielle to act as the landlord.

6. Danielle advertised the house for rent online. She subsequently rented the home to a man who used the house as the center of an illegal gambling ring. Danielle knows that the home is being used for that purpose, but does not inform Jeremy.
What is Danielle obligated to do given her knowledge of the activities happening at the house?
   A. Danielle has a duty to vacate the premises.
   B. Danielle, as the landlord, must make an application of removal of the tenant.
   C. Danielle is obligated to evict the tenants using brute force.
   D. Danielle is obligated to inform the local court of the activities taking place at the home.

7. Is Jeremy responsible for knowing how the rented property is being used?
   A. No, because Jeremy is not the landlord
   B. No, because Jeremy does not live near the property and has no way of knowing that the property is being used for illegal purposes
   C. Yes, because Jeremy can visit or drive by the property and clearly see it is used for illegal gambling purposes
   D. Yes, because Jeremy is the owner of the property

8. If Danielle does not bring an action to remove the tenants from the property, who is eligible to do so as if he/she is the owner of the property?
   A. Local law enforcement agency   B. Danielle's neighbors
   C. Jeremy's neighbors   D. The State of New York

9. After a final judgment for the landlord, the court shall issue a(n) _____ direct to the sheriff of the county or marshal of the city in which the property is situated, describing the property and commanding the officer to remove all persons.
   A. indictment   B. subpoena   C. warrant   D. summons

10. Court marshals appear at Bethany's apartment to execute the warrant for her eviction.
How much notice must the marshals provide Bethany?
_____ hours, excluding weekends and holidays.
   A. 24   B. 36   C. 72   D. 86

11. What effect does the warrant for an eviction have on the relationship between the landlord and tenant according to the New York Real Property Actions and Proceedings Law?
    The warrant _____ the landlord-tenant relationship.
    A. solidifies B. redeems C. rescinds D. cancels

12. Jason was served with a notice of petition for removal from his landlord, Eric. Jason has never been late on his rent, but has not paid Eric since his lease expired two months ago.
    May Jason respond to Eric's petition and, if so, how?
    A. No, Jason must vacate the premises immediately.
    B. Jason can respond, but only after he has vacated the premises.
    C. Jason can respond directly to Eric and record the conversation so that it can be preserved and presented to the court at a later date.
    D. Yes, Jason can prepare and file an answer to Eric's petition.

13. Assume the same facts as in Question 12. After Eric filed a notice of petition, the court decided it needs more information before moving on in the proceedings. In lieu of a notice of petition, the court may require which of the following?
    A. Order to show cause
    B. Specific description of the noise complaints or other grounds for eviction
    C. Payment receipts
    D. Formal complaint and deposition testimony

Questions 14-17.

DIRECTIONS: Questions 14 through 17 are to be answered on the basis of the following facts.

Dawn did not keep a copy of the lease her tenant, Mike, signed. Mike does not have a copy of the lease either. Mike maintains that the lease term has not expired, while Dawn says the lease ended a month ago.

14. At trial, the lease term is considered a
    A. fact in dispute   B. triable issue of fact
    C. respondent's contention   D. contentious fact

15. The apartment that Mike rents in Manhattan is in a building with eight other rental units. The court that hears the dispute between Dawn and Mike must first and foremost have
    A. contacts with Mike and Dawn   B. jurisdiction
    C. res ipsa   D. pro se litigant allowance

16. During the summary proceeding, the court's preliminary asks if there is any undisputed amount of rent owed. Assuming that Mike agrees that he is already behind one month of rent and Dawn agrees, who will the court direct Mike to deliver that rent payment to?
    A. The court for safekeeping
    B. An escrow account established by Mike, but put in Dawn's name
    C. An escrow account which names the County Clerk as the legal owner
    D. Directly to Dawn

17. The amount in dispute between Mike and Dawn is $5,000. Mike wants to countersue Dawn for $3,000; however, Mike refuses to deposit the disputed amount of money to the court. Mike has not paid any portion of the $5,000. Upon application, what actions can Dawn ask the court to take?
    A. Dismiss without prejudice Mike's counterclaims and defenses and grant judgment for Dawn
    B. Imprison Mike for non-payment of rent
    C. Garnish Mike's paychecks for the back payment of rent, and other arrears
    D. Restrict Mike's counterclaims as to only those relating to monetary damages

18. The term "constructive eviction" is defined as a(n)
    A. circumstance where the landlord does something or provides or, in the adverse, does not do something or fails to provide, that renders the property uninhabitable
    B. circumstance where the tenant deems the property uninhabitable and informs the landlord of the condition
    C. eviction notice that was served upon a tenant with a material defect
    D. illegitimate eviction, such as evicting the wrong occupant or eviction executed prior to proper service upon the tenant

19. If a stipulation is made between the parties in a special proceeding, other than a stipulation solely to adjourn or stay the proceeding, and either the petitioner or the respondent is not represented by counsel, the court shall
    A. fully describe the terms of the stipulation to that party
    B. accept the stipulation and record the stipulation in a deposition hearing
    C. reject the stipulation unless expressly consented to by both parties in writing
    D. continue with the hearing

20. An "undertenant" is also considered a(n)
    A. subtenant   B. overtenant   C. lessor   D. assignor

21. Upon proper proof of the existence of a condition that constructively evict the tenant from a portion of the premises that is likely to become dangerous to life, health or safety, the court before which the case is pending may _____ proceedings to dispossess the tenant for non-payment of rent.
    A. adjourn   B. joinder   C. stay   D. rectify

22. If service is mailed to the respondent for the notice of petition, service is deemed complete after which of the following events? 22.____
    A. Filing of the notice
    B. Filing the proof of service
    C. Commencement of the action
    D. Start of trial

Questions 23-25.

DIRECTIONS: Questions 23 through 25 are to be answered on the basis of the following passage.

In a proceeding to recover the possession of premises in the City of New York occupied for dwelling purposes upon the ground that the occupant is holding over and continuing in possession of the premises after the expiration of his term and without permission of the landlord may stay the issuance of a warrant and also stay an execution to collect the costs of proceeding for a period of not more than __1__ months, if it appears that the premises are used __2__ purposes; that the application is made in good faith; that the applicant cannot within the neighborhood secure suitable premises similar to those occupied by him and that he made __3__ efforts to secure such other premises, or that by reason of other facts it would occasion extreme hardship to him or his family if the stay were not granted.

23. Please fill in the number of months for Blank #1. 23.____
    A. one   B. two   C. six   D. eight

24. Please fill in the correct word for Blank #2. 24.____
    A. illegal   B. dwelling   C. illicit   D. residential

25. Please fill in the correct phrase for Blank #3. 25.____
    A. due and reasonable
    B. fair and reasonable
    C. reasonable and due
    D. reasonable and fair

KEY (CORRECT ANSWERS)

1. C
2. A
3. D
4. D
5. B

6. B
7. D
8. A
9. C
10. C

11. D
12. D
13. A
14. B
15. B

16. D
17. A
18. A
19. A
20. A

21. C
22. B
23. C
24. B
25. A

EXAMINATION SECTION
TEST 1

DIRECTIONS: Each question or incomplete statement is followed by several suggested answers or completions. Select the one that BEST answers the question or completes the statement. *PRINT THE LETTER OF THE CORRECT ANSWER IN THE SPACE AT THE RIGHT.*

1. Which of the following parties is authorized to administer oaths?   1.____
   A. All court clerks
   B. Court bailiffs
   C. Judges only
   D. Judge's clerks only

2. Janelle has been retained as Stephanie's defense attorney. Stephanie is charged with felony burglary in the first degree.   2.____
   When must Janelle file a notice of appearance with the court?
   A. Before opening argument
   B. Before her first appearance in court or 10 days after her appointment, whichever is sooner
   C. 10 days after her appointment as Stephanie's attorney
   D. No later than Stephanie's first scheduled arraignment

3. Tony is a new associate at the law offices of Deck & Decker, LLP. He needs to file a motion to dismiss for his managing attorney's client and is unsure of where to deliver the papers for the court's consideration.   3.____
   Unless directed to do directly by the court, papers for consideration of the court should be delivered to
   A. the presiding judge
   B. the clerk's office of the trial court in the appropriate courtroom
   C. any of the judges in the appropriate courtroom
   D. the bailiff or court officer on duty

4. How many terms of court are in one year?   4.____
   A. 12   B. 13   C. 26   D. 52

5. Upon otherwise excluded from a courtroom by the judge, the Family Court is open to the   5.____
   A. families having business in the court only
   B. extended families having business in the court only
   C. public
   D. judge's law clerks and court officers only

6. Which of the following is a factor the judge may consider in excluding someone from the courtroom during a Family Court proceeding?   6.____
   The person is
   A. causing or likely to cause a disruption in the proceedings
   B. related to a member of the family in the court
   C. related to the judge or other clerk
   D. an alternate court officer

2 (#1)

7. Which of the following are appropriate considerations for a pre-trial conference?
   A. Completion of discovery
   B. Admissions of fact
   C. Possibilities for settlement
   D. All of the above

   7.____

8. In any proceeding to determine temporary or permanent custody or visitation, once a hearing or trial is commenced, it shall proceed to conclusion within _____ days.
   A. 30   B. 60   C. 90   D. 120

   8.____

Questions 9-12.

DIRECTIONS: Questions 9 through 12 are to be answered on the basis of the following fact pattern.

Tim and Kat have two children together. After their divorce, Tim was ordered to pay child support in the amount of $480 per month. Soon after divorcing, Tim lost his job as a paralegal with a local law firm but quickly found another job that paid more than double his paralegal salary. Tim has not paid child support in over six months. Kat recently learned that Tim has been earning more than enough money to pay the monthly support obligation as well as the amount Tim owes in arrears.

9. What must Kat file in order to schedule a hearing to determine nonpayment of child support?
   A. A petition that alleges willful violation of an order of support
   B. A subpoena that requires Tim to hand over his bank statements
   C. A summons that requires Tim to hand over his bank statements
   D. A notice of deposition to inform Tim that a complaint will follow

   9.____

10. After the judge or support magistrate commences a hearing to determine whether Tim is purposefully evading paying child support, how many adjournments can each side request?
    A. Unlimited
    B. Up to two adjournments each
    C. Only one adjournment can be permitted, and only to secure counsel
    D. No adjournments are permitted

    10.____

11. The hearing must conclude within how many days of commencement?
    A. 30   B. 60   C. 90   D. 120

    11.____

12. Assume that testimony must be taken in the hearing between Tim and Kat. The testimony will be given by Tim's former employer, Bob, who has recently moved to Idaho.
    Can Bob provide testimony by telephone or other electronic means?
    A. Yes, with court approval and if the request is completed using an official form
    B. Yes, if Kat and Tim both consent to the method of testimony delivery

    12.____

48

C. Yes, if Kat and Tim both consent in writing at least fifteen days prior to the scheduled hearing date
D. No

13. Which of the following must be submitted with a petition to terminate the birth mother's rights?
    A. Sworn written statement by the mother naming the father
    B. A blood sample of the child's maternal grandmother
    C. A blood or other DNA sample of the child's paternal grandmother
    D. A sworn written statement by any individual familiar with both the mother and father who can attest to the identity of both parties

14. When a child is placed in foster care, he or she comes under the jurisdiction of the _____ Court.
    A. Surrogates   B. Civil   C. Criminal   D. Family

15. Judge Slater presided over the hearing regarding Baby Jay's foster care placement. In a subsequent proceeding, Baby Jay's mother has decided to voluntarily terminate her parental rights.
    Will Judge Slater be assigned to the parental rights hearing?
    A. No
    B. Yes, if practicable
    C. Yes, if specifically requested by Baby Jay's current guardian
    D. Yes, if specifically requested by the parent requesting her rights be terminated

16. If a child in a custody proceeding is Native American, that child is subject to which of the following?
    A. Social Services Law
    B. Indian Child Welfare Act
    C. Child Welfare Act of Natives
    D. Division of American Children

17. Which of the following papers is required in an adoption proceeding?
    A. Certified copy of the birth certificate of the adoptive child
    B. Certified marriage certificate, where the adoptive parents are married
    C. A proposed order of adoption
    D. All of the above

18. The court may determine the best interests of the child in an adoption proceeding factoring in which of the following?
    A. The sexual orientation of the adoptive parents
    B. The race or ethnicity of the adoptive parents
    C. The age of the adoptive child
    D. None of the above

19. At any scheduled call of a calendar or at any conference, if all parties do not appear, the court may note the _____ on the record.
    A. dismissal   B. acquittal
    C. acquiescence   D. default

20. In any discontinued action, the attorney for the defendant shall file a stipulation or statement of discontinuance with the county clerk within _____ day(s) of such continuance.
    A. one   B. ten   C. fifteen   D. twenty

21. Unless the court otherwise provides, where the attorney of record for any party arranges for another attorney to conduct the trial, the trial counsel must be identified in writing to the court and all parties no later than 15 days after the pretrial conference or, if there is not a pretrial conference, at least _____ days before trial.
    A. 10   B. 5   C. 15   D. 30

22. A preliminary examination of a witness or juror by a judge or counsel prior to trial is known as the process of
    A. de jure
    B. benchmarking
    C. voir dire
    D. stare decisis

23. Which two pieces of information are attorneys prohibited from sharing in the process identified in Question 22?
    Counsel may not
    A. read from any pleadings or information potential jurors of the amount of money at issue
    B. identify their client or provide any background to the dispute at issue
    C. reveal their true identities or provide any detail as to where the dispute at issue took place
    D. provide any details about the case but may provide details on the identity of their client

24. A bifurcated trial is MOST appropriate in which of the following circumstances?
    A. A bar owner serves alcohol to a minor and may be both criminally liable and civilly liable for the damages to the minor
    B. A disgruntled neighbor who yells at his neighbor and kicks over his garden gnomes is sued
    C. A civil dispute between Amy and her former employer has come to the surface after Amy accuses her employer of sexual harassment
    D. A dispute between friends that is settled outside of court

25. Each attorney appearing in a proceeding shall file a
    A. written notice of appearance
    B. written order of appearance
    C. oral notice of appearance
    D. written issue of notice

KEY (CORRECT ANSWERS)

1.	A		11.	B
2.	B		12.	A
3.	B		13.	A
4.	B		14.	D
5.	C		15.	B
6.	A		16.	B
7.	D		17.	D
8.	C		18.	D
9.	A		19.	D
10.	C		20.	D

21. A
22. C
23. A
24. A
25. A

TEST 2

DIRECTIONS: Each question or incomplete statement is followed by several suggested answers or completions. Select the one that BEST answers the question or completes the statement. *PRINT THE LETTER OF THE CORRECT ANSWER IN THE SPACE AT THE RIGHT.*

1. Mark wants to postpone determination of his visitation rights to see his daughter, Maddie. He believes he has a better chance of getting to see Maddie more if he lives within an hour of Maddie's mother and Mark is not moving until the end of next month.
   Generally, what is the time limitation on custody and/or visitation determination once a hearing is commenced?
   A. 30 days B. 60 days C. 90 days D. 120 days

   1.____

2. Which party assigns criminal actions to judges?
   A. Chief Justice of the New York Supreme Court
   B. Nassau County Supreme Court
   C. The Presiding Judge in the district of jurisdiction
   D. The Chief Administrator of the Courts

   2.____

3. A _____ of court is a designated unit of the court in which specified business of the court is to be conducted by a judge or quasi-judicial officer.
   A. unit B. division C. part D. sequence

   3.____

4. Tim has escaped from the Child Center in Albany. When a child absconds from a facility to which he or she was duly remanded, what action must an authorized representative of the facility take?
   Written notice must be given to the clerk of the court from which the remand was made within _____ hours.
   A. 24 B. 36 C. 48 D. 72

   4.____

5. Which of the following individuals is qualified to serve as a Support Magistrate?
   A. Margaret, a senior paralegal with the Utica Family Court
   B. Jamal, a former court bailiff who has been an acting family law attorney for the last six years
   C. Sharon, a Colorado criminal court chief justice
   D. Amy, a New York City police officer who is family with child custody issues

   5.____

6. Support magistrates shall be appointed as nonjudicial employees of the Unified Court System on a full-time basis for a term of _____ years and, in the discretion of the Chief Administrator, may be reappointed for a subsequent _____-year terms.
   A. 1; 2 B. 3; 5 C. 3; 3 D. 3; 6

   6.____

52

7. Ed and Elizabeth were married for eight years and four children together. Ed filed for divorce, alleging that Elizabeth had an affair with one of Ed's coworkers, Tom. Ed is seeking full custody of all four children and wants the court to deny Elizabeth alimony and child support.
Which of the following statements is a finding of fact?
   A. Elizabeth is most likely having an affair with Tom.
   B. Elizabeth is more than likely an adulterous spouse.
   C. Ed and Elizabeth were married for eight years.
   D. Elizabeth's request for child support is frivolous.

8. A certified copy of the birth certificate of the child must accompany which of the following hearings?
   A. An adoption proceeding
   B. Petition to terminate a birth mother's rights
   C. Extra-judicial surrender of a child
   D. All of the above

9. Which of the following qualify as a "special application" which must be made in writing and accompanied by affidavits setting forth the reason(s) for the application?
   A. Dispense with the statutorily required personal appearance
   B. Period of residence of a child
   C. Period of waiting after filing of the adoption petition
   D. All of the above

10. Rachel, a probation officer, has been asked to conduct an investigation into the guardianship of McKenzie, a recently orphaned four-year-old girl, in foster care. The court would like to appoint a guardian but needs a disinterested person to interview McKenzie's next of kin before rendering a decision.
Is Rachel authorized to conduct such an investigation?
    A. No, because Rachel is not an attorney
    B. No, because Rachel is not a certified private investigator
    C. Yes, because Rachel is presumably over the age of 18
    D. Yes, because an investigation by a disinterested person is authorized if requested by the court

11. When a petition for temporary guardianship has been filed by an adoptive parent, the clerk of the court in which the petition has been filed shall distribute a written notice to the adoptive parents and lawyers who have appeared, and to the Commissioner of _____ or the Director of the _____, as appropriate.
    A. Mental Health; Family Court
    B. Court Services; Child Welfare Services
    C. Social Services; Probation Service
    D. Social Services; Family Court Services

12. Bella would like to terminate her parental rights and surrender her daughter to foster care. Bella, however, is unsure of how to proceed and is nervous to speak with any of the court officers or court clerks. Bella currently lives in Utica County, New York.
Which of the following individuals is designated to speak with Bella about bringing a proceeding under the Family Court Act before the proceeding is commenced?
    A. Commanding officer of any law enforcement agency providing police service in Utica County
    B. Utica County district attorney
    C. The clerk of the Family Court and the clerk of the criminal court of Utica County
    D. All of the above

12._____

Questions 13-15.

DIRECTIONS: Questions 13 through 15 are to be answered on the basis of the following fact pattern.

James is sixteen and does not attend school. He continuously disobeys his parents and has been caught selling drugs from his parent's home on at least one occasion.

13. James MOST likely qualifies as a(n)
    A. incarcerated person
    B. person in need of supervision
    C. indemnified individual
    D. indigent prisoner

13._____

14. May James' parents hire an attorney to represent James?
    A. No, the attorney will represent James and his parents wholly
    B. No, James must be proven guilty before an attorney can be appointed
    C. No, there is no such "Attorney for Child" concept in New York State
    D. Yes

14._____

15. James sold cocaine from his parent's apartment to an acquaintance of his from his old school. The buyer of the drugs, Sam, died of an overdose. Sam's parents have sued James. How is a court case against James commenced?
    A. Sam's parents must file a PINS petition in Family Court.
    B. A subpoena must be served on James' parents.
    C. An indictment must be filed in the county where the commission of the crime occurred or, in this case, in the county where James' parents reside.
    D. Discovery demands should be fulfilled by both sides before an action can be commenced.

15._____

16. Proceedings for adoption from an authorized agency shall be calendared within _____ days of the filing of the petition to review said petition and determine if there is an adequate basis for approving the adoption.
    A. 20   B. 30   C. 45   D. 60

16._____

17. Assume the same facts as in Question 16. The court shall schedule the appearance of the adoptive parent(s) and the child before the court, for approval of the adoption within _____ days of the date of the review.
    A. 20　　　　　B. 30　　　　　C. 45　　　　　D. 60

17._____

18. Is there a time limit for proceedings involving custody or visitation?
    A. Yes, once a hearing or trial is commenced, it must proceed to conclusion within 90 days
    B. Yes, once a hearing or trial is commenced, it must proceed to conclusion within 120 days
    C. No, as each case must be determined by the specific fact pattern presented to the court
    D. No, unless there is a petition from either party to expedite the proceeding

18._____

19. Admissions of fact, fixing a date for fact-finding and dispositional hearings are most appropriately confined to a
    A. pre-trial conference
    B. subpoena conference
    C. disposition hearing
    D. engagement of counsel determination

19._____

20. Which of the following individuals is LEAST likely to be permitted to access the pleadings of a Family Court case?
    A. A child who is a party to a proceeding
    B. Parents who are legally responsible for the care of the child subject to a proceeding
    C. A reporter for the New York Ledger
    D. An authorized representative of the child protective agency involved in the proceeding

20._____

21. The general public or any person may be excluded from a Family Court courtroom only if the judge presiding in the courtroom determines, on a case-by-case basis such exclusion
    A. is warranted in that case
    B. would prejudice the rights of the child
    C. would prejudice the rights of the parents
    D. would bring negative press to either party's attorney

21._____

22. Which of the following two documents are provided by the Family Court to assist in filing an appeal?
    A. Request for Appellate Division Intervention Form; Notice of Appeal
    B. Subpoena Request Form; Notice of Appeal
    C. Request for Appellate Division Intervention Form; Order of Appeal
    D. Order of Appeal; Notice of Appeal

22._____

23. The _____ shall conduct preliminary conferences with any person seeking to have a juvenile delinquency petition filed, concerning the advisability of requesting that a juvenile delinquency petition be filed and in order to gather information needed for a determination of the suitability of the case for adjustment.
    A. Chief Judicial Administrator
    B. Probation Service
    C. Court Clerk
    D. Family Services

24. Can hearings be recorded?
    A. No
    B. Not unless all parties consent in writing at least 60 days prior to arraignment
    C. Not unless the court's clerk approves
    D. yes

25. John's hearing to determine whether he is willfully not paying child support is scheduled for Tuesday morning. On Monday night, John becomes extremely ill with food poisoning.
    Will John's hearing be adjourned?
    A. No, under no circumstances will a hearing for willful nonpayment be adjourned
    B. No, unless the court's clerk is able to communicate John's illness to the court within 24 hours of the hearing
    C. Yes, if the court bailiff consents to the adjournment
    D. Yes, the hearing may be adjourned for illness of a party or other good cause

KEY (CORRECT ANSWERS)

1. C
2. D
3. C
4. C
5. B

6. B
7. C
8. D
9. D
10. D

11. C
12. D
13. B
14. D
15. A

16. D
17. B
18. A
19. A
20. C

21. A
22. A
23. B
24. D
25. D

EXAMINATION SECTION

TEST 1

DIRECTIONS: Each question or incomplete statement is followed by several suggested answers or completions. Select the one that BEST answers the question or completes the statement. *PRINT THE LETTER OF THE CORRECT ANSWER IN THE SPACE AT THE RIGHT.*

1. A "person acting as a parent" is defined as a person who has physical custody or has had physical custody for a period of _____ months, including any temporary absence, within one year immediately before the commencement of a child custody proceeding and has been awarded legal custody by a court or claims a right to legal custody under the law of this state.
   A. four concurrent
   B. six consecutive
   C. eight consecutive
   D. ten concurrent

   1.____

2. Samantha and her son, Gary, spend the summer months with her parents in North Dakota. During the school year, however, Samantha returns to New York. Samantha's child custody case with Gary's father has been ongoing in New York for over eight months.
   Should the custody case be heard in North Dakota or New York?
   A. North Dakota, since Gary spends a significant amount of time there during the year
   B. North Dakota, unless Gary's father objects for reasonable cause
   C. North Dakota, but only if Samantha petitions the court in New York and obtains the required permissions
   D. New York

   2.____

3. If a court declines to exercise jurisdiction over a child custody hearing because it determines that a court of a different state is a more appropriate forum, the court is said to have raised the issue of a(n)
   A. indeterminate venue
   B. inconvenient venue
   C. inconvenient forum
   D. indeterminate jurisdiction

   3.____

4. A warrant to take physical custody of a child may be executed in which of the following scenarios?
   A. Imminent risk of suffering serious physical harm
   B. Removal from the state
   C. Imminent risk of death
   D. All of the above

   4.____

5. Even though the Family Court does not have jurisdiction to modify a child custody determination, it may issue a temporary order to enforce which of the following?
   A. Visitation schedule made by another state
   B. Permanent child custody order finalized in another state
   C. Alimony payment schedule finalized in another state
   D. Child support payment arrangement schedule finalized in another state

   5.____

6. According to the New York Domestic Relations Law, a law enforcement officer may take any lawful action _____ necessary to locate a child.
   A. legally   B. reasonably   C. absolutely   D. willfully

Questions 7-10.

DIRECTIONS: Questions 7 through 10 are to be answered on the basis of the following facts.

Mike is planning on moving to New York with his two children, Emma and Courtney. Mike wants to ensure that the child custody determination that was finalized in Virginia between he and his ex-wife, Jill, is recognized in New York.

7. What can Mike do to ensure the courts in New York are notified of the final order?
   A. Stop by his local courthouse and speak to a clerk
   B. Send a certified letter to the local police station to notify them that the order is in place
   C. Request to register the child custody determination in New York State
   D. E-mail the Manhattan Family Court division requesting a personal meeting to outline the order

8. Assume that Mike has properly informed the New York courts of the child custody determination in Virginia. Jill is informed of Mike's actions by notice, but disagrees that the child custody agreement is final.
   Can Jill contest the filing?
   A. Yes, but only if she receives Mike's consent to contest
   B. Yes, but only if their children, Emma and Courtney, live with Jill at least full-time
   C. Yes, she may contest and request a hearing to contest the validity of the determination within twenty days of service of notice
   D. No

9. Under what grounds can Jill contest the validity of Mike's filing?
   A. The court in Virginia that presided over the hearing did not have jurisdiction over the child custody determination.
   B. The order Mike filed was vacated, stayed or modified by a court with proper jurisdiction.
   C. Jill was not properly served.
   D. Any of the above

10. If Jill disagrees that the child custody agreement is final, but ignores the service of notice, what are the consequences?
    A. Jill's rights to Emma and Courtney are deemed waived.
    B. Mike's filing is confirmed as a matter of law and Jill will be notified of this confirmation by service.
    C. Jill will need to make her late request in person in New York.
    D. Mike can formally request the court to waive Jill's parental rights.

11. Suppose that Amy had legal and physical custody over her niece, Rebecca, for the first three years of Rebecca's life. Amy is moving to Wyoming for work and consequently can no longer maintain physical custody of Rebecca. Can the courts depose, or take, Amy's testimony for the custody hearings over the phone?

    A. Yes, if Amy lives in another state and the record is preserved appropriately
    B. No, because Amy is not otherwise incapacitated and is capable of making herself available to a New York court
    C. No, unless the court receives permission from the successor legal guardian
    D. No

    11._____

12. Unless the court enters a temporary emergency order, the enforcing court may not stay an order enforcing a child custody determination pending

    A. requests otherwise B. adjudication
    C. appeal   D. abdication

    12._____

13. In a lengthy and contentious child custody case, John and Liz have accumulated enormous legal bills and other debts. Liz is ultimately the prevailing party in the case.
    What costs can the court impose upon John?

    A. None, as Liz cannot be reimbursed for legal fees in a child custody case
    B. Liz's legal fees only
    C. Necessary and reasonable expenses incurred including attorney's fees and travel expenses
    D. All of Liz's expenses incurred during the hearings and trial, including her meals

    13._____

14. A child custody determination was finalized between Amal and Jack in Lebanon. Jack petitions the court to vacate the order as it is invalid in New York. Jack ultimately would like to come to a new agreement between he and Amal regarding visitation.
    The court will treat the order from the Lebanese court as

    A. not binding, since neither Jack nor Amal live in Lebanon anymore
    B. binding, or otherwise as if the Lebanese court was a part of the United States
    C. binding, for a period of 90 days
    D. binding, for a period of up to one year or until both parents establish New York residency, whichever is longer

    14._____

15. Jamal is having difficulty getting along with his son's mother, Tanya. Jamal tells his friend, Chris, who happens to be an assistant district attorney, that Tanya prevents Jamal from seeing his son. Can Chris represent Jamal in a child custody modification hearing against Tanya?

    A. No
    B. Not unless Tanya consents
    C. Not unless the court consents
    D. Yes, but only in a non-binding arbitration forum

    15._____

16. The New York Domestic Relations Law does not apply to which two situations involving a child?
    A. Emergency medical care and surrogacy
    B. Adoption and guardianship
    C. College education expenses and surrogacy
    D. Emergency medical care and adoption

16._____

17. Baby Jane was abandoned on Interstate 95 on the New York side of the New Jersey border. After being discovered, the Manhattan Family Court ordered the baby to the custody of the New York Department of Child Services. Baby Jane's father, a New Jersey resident, discovered the baby had been abducted and demanded the baby be returned to his care, arguing the Manhattan Court did not have jurisdiction over the matter.
Did the Manhattan Court have jurisdiction?
    A. No, because Baby Jane's closest kin is an out-of-state resident
    B. No, because Baby Jane could have been left on the New Jersey side of the border
    C. Yes, because Baby Jane was found on the New York side of the border
    D. Yes, because Baby Jane was abandoned in the state

17._____

18. What issue, according to the New York Domestic Relations Law, must be handled expeditiously and given priority on the court's calendar in child custody cases if raised?
    A. Alimony
    B. Jurisdiction
    C. Registration of final orders
    D. Guardianship

18._____

19. A child custody proceeding that pertains to an Indian child is not subject to Article 5-A of the New York Domestic Relations Law to the extent that is governed by the
    A. Indian Sovereignty provisions
    B. Twentieth Amendment
    C. Indian Child Welfare Act
    D. Child Welfare and Indian Commitments Act

19._____

20. Before a child custody determination can be made, which two processes must be completed?
Service of notice and
    A. an opportunity to be heard
    B. establishment of jurisdiction
    C. filing of a complaint
    D. filing of a subpoena

20._____

21. Cynthia has physical custody over her daughter with her ex-wife, Mary. For child custody hearings, is Cynthia required to appear to the hearings with her daughter?
    A. The court may require Cynthia to appear in person with the child.
    B. Cynthia is always required to appear in person with the child.
    C. Cynthia is only allowed to appear with the child if Mary is given proper notice of the child's appearance
    D. Cynthia is not required under any circumstances to appear, even if the court requests so.

21._____

Questions 22-23.

DIRECTIONS: Questions 22 and 23 are to be answered on the basis of the following facts.

Sean and Erica want to modify their child custody determination. Sean and Erica lived in Florida for eight years before moving to New York. Their daughter, Brenda, was conceived in Florida and is now five years old, living with Erica full time.

22. The FIRST step in modifying a child custody determination is to
    A. serve Sean and Erica with proper notice and demand Erica appear in court with Brenda
    B. evaluate the current order to determine whether custody is split equally between both parents
    C. determine whether a proceeding to enforce a child custody determination has begun in another state
    D. allow Sean and Erica to make a formal request for modification by entering motion

22.____

23. If a proceeding to enforce a child custody determination has begun in another state, the court in New York may do which of the following?
    A. Continue with the modification hearing under conditions the court deems appropriate
    B. Ignore the other state's determination regardless of the outcome
    C. Request that both parties return to Florida to finish the proceeding
    D. Require that the child appear in court and ask the child which court's decision will be in her best interest

23.____

24. In the first pleading to the court, a party must know which of the following information?
    A. Child's present address
    B. Places where the child has lived in the last five years
    C. The names and addresses of the individuals that lived with the child in the last five years
    D. All of the above

24.____

25. In a child custody determination, each party has an affirmative duty to
    A. inform the court of any proceeding that will affect the current proceeding
    B. notify the court of a change in the child's mental or physical condition
    C. inform the court of a potential change in address for either party
    D. notify the court of a change in the party's legal representation

25.____

KEY (CORRECT ANSWERS)

1.	B	11.	A
2.	D	12.	C
3.	C	13.	C
4.	D	14.	B
5.	A	15.	A
6.	B	16.	D
7.	C	17.	D
8.	D	18.	B
9.	D	19.	C
10.	B	20.	A

21.	A
22.	C
23.	A
24.	D
25.	A

EXAMINATION SECTION
TEST 1

DIRECTIONS: Each question or incomplete statement is followed by several suggested answers or completions. Select the one that BEST answers the question or completes the statement. *PRINT THE LETTER OF THE CORRECT ANSWER IN THE SPACE AT THE RIGHT.*

1. A putative father is generally defined as
   A. a man who claims or is alleged to be the father of a child whom is not married to the child's mother at the time of birth
   B. a man who is the father of the child but does not sign the birth certificate
   C. a man who is the alleged father of the child based on the fact that he is married to the child's mother at the time of the child's birth
   D. the child's presumptive father at law

   1._____

2. Which of the following people are entitled to notice to proceedings?
   A. Person identified as the father in a sworn written statement by the mother
   B. Any person recorded on the birth certificate as the child's father
   C. Any person adjudicated by the court as the child's father
   D. All of the above

   2._____

3. James is listed as the father on Bella's birth certificate, but has been twice convicted of rape in the second degree. Bella is the result of rape.
   Is James entitled to receive notice of Bella's guardianship hearing?
   A. Yes, because he is the legal father
   B. Yes, because he signed the birth certificate as the father
   C. Yes, unless Bella's mother objects to James receiving notice
   D. No

   3._____

4. A surrender for adoption executed by a parent, parents or guardian who is in foster care shall be executed only before a judge of the _____ court.
   A. surrogates   B. family   C. civil   D. probate

   4._____

5. Bill and Joel are both possible fathers to Diana's newborn baby. Diana only invited Bill to the hospital and he subsequently signed the birth certificate. After the birth, however, Bill lost contact with Diana. Joel has taken care of the baby since the child's birth.
   Who is the presumed father of Diana's baby?
   A. Bill
   B. Joel
   C. Whomever Diana designates as the father
   D. Whichever man Diana names in a sworn written statement as the father

   5._____

6. Which of the following is NOT listed as finding of legislative intent? 6._____
   A. Is it desirable for children to grow up with a normal family life in a permanent home
   B. It is generally desirable for the child to remain with or be returned to the birth parent because the child's need for a normal family life will usually best be met in the home of its birth parent, and that parents are entitled to bring up their own children unless the best interests of the child would be thereby endangered
   C. It is desirable for the child to live in one residence until the age of majority with both parents
   D. The state's first obligation is to help the family with services to prevent its break-up or to reunite if the child has already left home

7. The term "child" shall mean a person under the age of _____ years. 7._____
   A. sixteen   B. eighteen   C. twenty-one   D. twenty-five

Questions 8-9.

DIRECTIONS: Questions 8 and 9 are to be answered on the basis of the following passage from the New York Social Services Law.

"Permanently neglected child" shall mean a child who is in the care of an authorized agency and whose parent or custodian has failed for a period of either at least _____ or fifteen out of the most recent twenty-two months following the date such child came into the care of an authorized agency substantially and continuously or repeatedly to maintain contact with or plan for the future of the child, although physically and financially able to do so, notwithstanding the agency's diligent efforts to encourage and strengthen the parental relationship when such efforts will not be detrimental to the best interests of the child."

8. Please fill in the blank. 8._____
   A. one year   B. two years   C. three years   D. four years

9. The New York City agency tasked with ensuring the welfare of children and their families is called 9._____
   A. State of Children's Welfare Agency
   B. Administration for Children's Services
   C. Department of Child Welfare
   D. Agency of Family Services and Children's Needs

10. Rachel was placed in the home of her adoptive parents last July. What date is used to record the placement? 10._____
    A. The date of the adoption agreement will be recorded in a bound volume maintained by the agency along with the names of the adoptive parents
    B. The date the child moves into the home of the adoptive parents
    C. The date the child agrees to move into the home of the adoptive parents
    D. The date the adoptive parents agree to adopt a child

11. Surrenders must be written and can be either _____.
    A. jurisdictional or extra-territorial   B. judicial or extra-judicial
    C. judicial or ex-parte   B. jurisdictional or extra-judicial

12. In cases where a surrender is not executed and acknowledged before a judge, the authorized agency to which the child was surrendered shall file an application for approval in which court?
    A. The court in which the adoption proceeding is expected to be filed or, if not known, the family or surrogates court in the county in which the agency has its principal office
    B. The family or surrogates court in the county where the child was born
    C. The family or surrogates court in the county where the child was raised for the first eighteen months of life
    D. The court in which the adoption proceeding was already filed

13. Which of the following is NOT required to be stated in the affidavit accompanying the surrender?
    A. Date, time, and place where the surrender was executed and acknowledged
    B. A written statement that the parent was provided with ha copy of the surrender
    C. A statement that the parent executed and acknowledged the surrender
    D. A statement that the child executed and acknowledged the surrender

14. Katie is fifteen years old. Before Katie can be committed to the guardianship and custody of foster care, which of the following is MOST likely to occur at a court proceeding?
    A. The child care agency will likely provide proof of the likelihood the child will be adopted.
    B. The court may, in its discretion, consider Katie's wishes in determining who would be promoted by the commitment or guardianship
    C. The child's parents' wishes will be a strong consideration and the court will author a separate opinion on the matter
    D. The potential adoptive parents will be deposed so that a sworn, written statement can accompany Katie's permanent file with the court

Questions 15-16.

DIRECTIONS: Questions 15 and 16 are to be answered on the basis of the following passage.

The date of the child's entry into foster care is the earlier of __1__ days after the date on which the child was removed from the home or the date the child was found by a court to be an abused or neglected child pursuant to Article 10 of the __2__ Act.

15. Fill in the number of days for Blank #1.
    A. 20   B. 30   C. 60   D. 80

16. Fill in the name of the act for Blank #2.
    A. Family Court
    B. Child Welfare
    C. Emancipated Child
    D. Surrogates

17. Carol and Tom want to sign the surrender to terminate their parental rights of their child, but cannot afford an attorney.
    May they request the court to appoint a lawyer on their behalf free of charge?
    A. No, because Carol and Tom must pay for their own attorney
    B. No, because Carol and Tom are initiating the proceeding
    C. No, because Carol and Tom do not need an attorney to execute a surrender
    D. Yes

18. What rights does a parent forfeit in a surrender, unless different terms are specifically agreed to?
    A. The right to visit the child
    B. The right to write to or otherwise learn about the child
    C. The right to speak to the child
    D. All of the above

19. Where will the surrender be recorded?
    In the office of the county clerk where the
    A. surrender is executed
    B. child was born
    C. biological parents reside
    D. adoptive parents reside

20. Can the executed surrender which places a child in the custody of an authorized agency also be used to commit the same child to the custody of the child's maternal grandparents?
    A. Yes, because they are in the same bloodline
    B. Yes, because a surrender operates to place the child anywhere the child is safe
    C. No, because the surrender is deemed to only apply to the commitment to the authorized agency; any other document is not deemed a surrender
    D. No, because the surrender cannot be re-executed or re-signed after the authorized agency signs the document

21. May the court disapprove a surrender?
    A. No, once executed the court cannot nullify the document
    B. No, because the court does not have the authority to disapprove a surrender
    C. Yes, and if the court does so the surrender is deemed resigned
    D. Yes, and if the court does so the surrender is deemed nullified

22. The _____ is a state level legal option for unmarried males to document through a notary public any female they engage in intercourse, for the purpose of retaining parental rights for any child they may father.
    A. pool of potential fathers
    B. putative father registry
    C. unmarried father registry
    D. putative biological dad registry

23. What is the purpose of a permanency hearing?
    A. To determine in which county a child should reside
    B. To determine the best interests of the child and develop a permanent plan for the placement of the child
    C. To develop a plan to determine the best interests of the child in three-year increments
    D. To schedule parties to testify on behalf of the child

24. When must the first permanency hearing be scheduled relative to when the place in the custody of the authorized agency, and thereafter how often must they continue thereafter?
    _____ months after the child is placed and every _____ thereafter.
    A. 8; 6 months   B. 6; month   C. 9; 5 months   D. 10; 2 months

25. Which of the following are possible options for disposition of the child after the fact-finding hearing?
    A. Releasing the child to the parents or guardian with supervision from the child protective agency
    B. Placing the child in foster care for a period of time
    C. Suspended judgment
    D. All of the above

KEY (CORRECT ANSWERS)

1.	A	11.	B
2.	D	12.	A
3.	D	13.	D
4.	B	14.	B
5.	A	15.	C
6.	C	16.	A
7.	B	17.	D
8.	A	18.	D
9.	B	19.	A
10.	A	20.	C

21.	D
22.	B
23.	B
24.	A
25.	D

EXAMINATION SECTION

TEST 1

DIRECTIONS: Each question or incomplete statement is followed by several suggested answers or completions. Select the one that BEST answers the question or completes the statement. *PRINT THE LETTER OF THE CORRECT ANSWER IN THE SPACE AT THE RIGHT.*

1. Forcible touching is classified as a
   A. Class A Misdemeanor
   B. Class B Misdemeanor
   C. Class C Misdemeanor
   D. Felony

   1.____

2. Inciting to riot is classified as a
   A. Class B Misdemeanor
   B. Grand Felony
   C. Class A Misdemeanor
   D. Felony

   2.____

3. A misdemeanor is defined as an offense, other than a traffic infraction, for which a sentence to a term of imprisonment in excess of _____ day(s) may be imposed, but for which a sentence to a term of imprisonment in excess of _____ year(s) cannot be imposed.
   A. six; one   B. five; one   C. fifteen; two   D. fifteen; one

   3.____

4. Fortune telling, falser personation and creating a hazard are all classified as
   A. felonies
   B. misdemeanors
   C. violations
   d. minor infractions

   4.____

5. A motorist, Jan, ran a traffic light at the intersection of Buffalo Avenue and Rochester Way. Jan is afraid that she has committed a misdemeanor because she was applying lipstick as she was driving and nearly hit a fire hydrant after she realized she blew the light.
   What is Jan guilty of committing?
   A. A traffic infraction, which is not a misdemeanor
   B. A traffic infraction, also known as a misdemeanor
   C. A Class A Misdemeanor
   D. A Class B Misdemeanor

   5.____

6. If James is sentenced to a period of probation, which of the following is MOST likely to accompany the sentence?
   A. The conditions of the sentence, including not leaving the state or abstaining from alcohol
   B. The address of James's probation officer and how to get there from James's home address
   C. The address of the judge presiding over James's probation hearing
   D. The jury instructions which were given to the jury in James's trial

   6.____

7. For a Class A Misdemeanor, other than sexual assault, what is the MAXIMUM period of probation?
   A. Two years   B. Three years   C. Four years   D. Five years

8. For a Class A Misdemeanor sexual assault, the period of probation is _____ years.
   A. four   B. five   C. six   D. seven

9. The conditions of probation or conditional discharge shall be determined by the
   A. jury
   B. parole officer
   C. court
   D. prosecuting attorney

10. When imposing a sentence of probation or conditional discharge, the court may consider restitution and require which of the following?
    A. The defendant avoid injurious habits
    B. Work in a respectable retail environment
    C. Study to become a nurse or other healthcare professional
    D. Participate in an alcohol or substance abuse program of the defendant's family's choosing

11. If Bill has been convicted of a traffic violation which caused the serious physical injury or death of another person, which of the following may the court require as a condition of probation?
    A. Anger management course
    B. Motor vehicle accident prevention course
    C. Defense driving course
    D. Motor skills and research methodology course

12. Unconditional discharge may be imposed for a felony as long as the court sets forth the
    A. actions the defendant has taken not to repeat his or her illicit behavior
    B. reasons for its actions
    C. skills or other licenses of the defendant
    D. other crimes the defendant is alleged to have committed

13. Pursuant to Article 65 of the New York Penal Law, as a condition of probation for sex offenders, the court may impose which of the following additional conditions?
    Reasonable limitation on
    A. food obtained from local grocery stores
    B. his or her use of the internet
    C. the amount of money expended on gaming devices
    D. extracurricular activities

14. Pursuant to Article 70 of the New York Penal Law, the court must inquire that parents of a minor committed to the Department of Corrections grant the minor the capacity to consent to
    A. routine dental treatment
    B. mental health treatment, but only if needed
    C. routine medical treatment, but only if required
    D. routine medical, dental, and mental health services and treatment

15. If a defendant is given a sentence of life imprisonment without parole, where will the defendant be committed?
    A. Custody of the City Department of Corrections
    B. Custody of the State Department of Corrections
    C. Custody of the State Department of Corrections and community supervisions for the remainder of the life of the defendant
    D. Rikers Island

16. A court sentence may run
    A. concurrently or consecutively
    B. concurrently or contemporaneously
    C. consecutively or respectively
    D. concurrently or coincidentally

17. Rich has been convicted of a felony murder of his cousin, Eric. While released on $5,000,000 bail, he is alleged to have murdered a shopkeeper in Albany. Rich is convicted of 25 years for the murder of Eric and 30 years for the murder of the shopkeeper. The sentences will run _____ for a total of _____ years incarceration.
    A. consecutively; 30
    B. consecutively; 55
    C. concurrently; 55
    D. contemporaneously; 30

Questions 18-19.

DIRECTIONS: Questions 18 and 19 are to be answered on the basis of the following information.

Paul and Amy have filed for divorce. Amy has been granted $450 per month in alimony, but Paul has not paid in over seven months. Amy has been living with her sister, Meredith, for over a year and because Paul has not paid Amy alimony, Amy has not been able to pay Meredith rent.

18. May Meredith petition the court to enforce the judgment against Paul?
    A. Yes, because Meredith is materially affected by Paul's nonpayment.
    B. Yes, because Meredith is Amy's sibling and thereby part of her nuclear family.
    C. No, because Amy has only been living with Meredith for a part of Paul's period of noncompliance with the court order.
    D. No.

19. A petition to enforce the judgment against Paul would need to be brought   19.____
    in which court?
    A. State of New York
    B. Supreme Court or a Court of Competent Jurisdiction
    C. Manhattan Family Court
    D. Criminal Court

20. During a support proceeding in family court, which of the following will   20.____
    MOST likely be accompanied to a sworn statement of net worth?
    A. Pay stubs from the year the individual earned the most, and the least,
       amount of money
    B. Tax return without any accompanying documentation
    C. W-2 tax and wage statements
    D. Current paycheck stub, most recently filed income tax returns, and the
       W-2 wage and income statements

Questions 21-22.

DIRECTIONS: Questions 21 and 22 are to be answered on the basis of the following
              information.

Candace filed for divorce from Jason last January. Jason and Candace have agreed to a support arrangement between themselves. Jason will pay Candace $300 per month, except during the summer months of June, July, and August, when Jason is temporarily out of work due to his occupation as a teaching paraprofessional.

21. What must Candace produce to the Court for approval?   21.____
    A. The agreement itself which must be reduced to writing
    B. Jason's bank statements, proving he can afford to pay $300 per month
    C. Jason's pay stubs, proving he is customarily out of work during the
       summer months
    D. The agreement is automatically approved given that the parties arranged
       the details themselves.

22. Who will approve the document Candace produces to the Court?   22.____
    A. The jury
    B. The attorney(s) representing Jason
    C. The court only
    D. The court or support magistrate

23. A summons was served on Jamal requiring him to appear for a family   23.____
    court proceeding involving his sister and father. Jamal failed to appear. The
    court may issue a(n) _____ directing that Jamal be arrested and brought before
    the court.
    A. indictment   B. subpoena   C. issue   D. warrant

24. With respect to the finding of the court and according to the New York Family Court Act, the effect of the issuance of a temporary order of protection is
    A. essentially a finding of guilt
    B. admission by the parties that the defendant will harm his or herself and others
    C. not a finding of wrongdoing
    D. a precursor to a felony conviction

24.____

25. Assume that a warrant is issued for Daniel in Richmond County. Where will Daniel be taken if he is taken into custody in Suffolk County?
    A. A family judge in Suffolk County
    B. A family judge in Richmond County
    C. A family judge in New York City
    D. The Supreme Court

25.____

KEY (CORRECT ANSWERS)

1.	A		11.	B
2.	C		12.	B
3.	D		13.	B
4.	B		14.	D
5.	A		15.	C
6.	A		16.	A
7.	B		17.	B
8.	C		18.	D
9.	C		19.	B
10.	A		20.	D

21.	A
22.	D
23.	D
24.	C
25.	A

TEST 2

DIRECTIONS: Each question or incomplete statement is followed by several suggested answers or completions. Select the one that BEST answers the question or completes the statement. *PRINT THE LETTER OF THE CORRECT ANSWER IN THE SPACE AT THE RIGHT.*

1. Which of the following is a defendant the LEAST likely to hear when being brought before the court pursuant to a warrant?
   He or she will be
   A. informed of the contents of the petition
   B. given the opportunity to present witnesses
   C. advised of their right to counsel
   D. given the option of having the public hear the case

   1._____

2. If the initial return of a summons or warrant is before a judge of the court, when support is an issue, the judge must make a(n) _____ order, either temporary or permanent with regard to support.
   A. reasonable   B. timely   C. immediate   D. seasoned

   2._____

3. Kevin has petitioned the court for temporary child support for his daughter, Maddie, from his ex-wife Katie. Katie objects to any determination of child support even though Maddie lives with Kevin full time. Katie argues that Kevin makes more money than her and there is no outstanding emergency or other issue that warrants the need for child support.
   May the court make an order for temporary child support?
   A. No, because Kevin earns more than Katie.
   B. No, because there is no impending emergency or issue warranting support.
   C. Yes, because Maddie lives with Kevin.
   D. Yes, because the court may make an order for temporary support sufficient to meet the needs of the child without a showing of immediate need.

   3._____

4. Dante is deemed an "eligible offender" because of his prior conviction of armed robbery. An eligible offender is an individual
   A. with a prior conviction
   B. with a prior conviction of a felony with a deadly weapon
   C. who has a prior conviction of an offense, but has not been convicted of more than once of a felony
   D. with at least one prior felony conviction

   4._____

5. How many votes are required from the State Board of Parole to issue a certificate of good conduct for an eligible offender?
   _____ unanimous votes
   A. Two   B. Three   C. Five   D. Four

   5._____

6. Jim is interested in obtaining a certificate of good conduct from the New York State Board of Parole after serving time for a Class C Felony.
   What is the MINIMUM amount of time that must pass before the Parole Board can grant Jim a certificate of good conduct, assuming he satisfies all other requirements of the Board?
   A. One year
   B. Eighteen months
   C. Two years
   D. Three years

   6.____

7. Leandra's Law specifies that no person shall operate a motor vehicle while impaired or otherwise intoxicated with a child aged _____ years or less as a passenger.
   A. twelve
   B. thirteen
   C. fifteen
   D. eighteen

   7.____'

8. Liam was convicted of driving under the influence of alcohol when he was nineteen in California, his home state. In an attempt to escape his license suspension of one year, he moved to New York to live with his aunt.
   Is Liam's license still suspended?
   A. Yes, his license is suspended in California only
   B. Yes, his license is suspended in New York and California
   C. Yes, his license is suspended in all states
   D. No

   8.____

9. An adult driving under the combination of drugs and alcohol for the first time will MOST likely be convicted of a
   A. traffic infraction
   B. sanction offense
   C. misdemeanor
   D. felony

   9.____

10. James has been hired as a marketing assistant for a local pharmaceutical company. After he received his offer letter from the Human Resources Department with his starting salary and start date, he received a call from Sylvia, the HR Coordinator. She informed James that a mistake had been made and the company did not realize James had a criminal record. She rescinded the employment offer and apologized to James for the inconvenience.
    Did the company violate any law?
    A. No, the company is permitted to rescind the offer since James is a felon
    B. No, the company informed James of the situation before he started his employment
    C. Yes, the company should have completed his background search prior to sending his offer of employment
    D. Yes

    10.____

11. Before Daniel started law school, he became a licensed HVAC technician working for his father's air conditioning repair business. After law school, he became a licensed attorney. Daniel also owns a handgun for which he has a permit. Which of the following are considered "licenses" under the New York Corrections Law Article 23-a?
    A. HVAC license only
    B. HVAC and Bar licenses only
    C. HVAC and Firearm licenses only
    D. HVAC, Bar and Firearm licenses

    11.____

12. When Marissa was 19, she began working for a local accountant, Bill. After one year as an intern, she began to steal cash and other gifts Bill received from his clients. Bill reported her to authorities and she was convicted of larceny. Seven years later, Marissa is denied employment as an accountant with a local CPA firm.
Why is this permitted under the New York Corrections Law?
   A. There is a direct relationship between the offense she committed and the employment she is seeking.
   B. Denial of employment is only permitted after ten years has passed since the conviction, not seven years.
   C. Marissa was not a minor when she committed the crime.
   D. The CPA firm is not permitted to deny Marissa employment in this situation.

12.____

13. Once a child custody determination has been decided, it is conclusive unless and until the
   A. parents move out of state
   B. child moves out of state with one of the parents
   C. order is modified or changed
   D. judge nullifies the order due to noncompliance

13.____

14. When Bob and Sharon were dating, they lived in Connecticut and moved to Westchester County after they got married. They had their son, Jayden, soon after and when Jayden turned six years old, Bob and Sharon divorced. Bob moved back to Connecticut and has petitioned the court for full legal and physical custody of Jayden. The child custody determination hearings have started in New York and Bob would like his sister, Michelle, to testify on his behalf at the hearing. Michelle lives in Connecticut.
May Bob's sister testify?
   A. No
   B. No, because she lives in Connecticut
   C. Yes, even though she lives in Connecticut
   D. Yes, because she is a material witness to Bob and Sharon's marriage

14.____

15. A private placement adoption is MOST accurately defined as any adoption
   A. of a minor other than that placed by an authorized agency
   B. organized by three or more parties
   C. of a minor organized directly by the parties of the adoptee child
   D. of a minor other than that placed by a government agency

15.____

16. James wants to adopt his stepdaughter, Stephanie, so that he can include her in his will. James is still married to Stephanie's mother, Diane.
May James adopt Stephanie?
   A. It cannot be determined because it is not known if Stephanie is a minor.
   B. Yes, because James has a legitimate reason for adopting Stephanie.
   C. No, because James requires Diane's signature or consent to adopt Stephanie.
   D. No, because James cannot adopt Stephanie for the purpose of inheritance or support rights.

16.____

17. Which of the following individuals will be entitled to notice of adoption pursuant to the New York Domestic Relations Law?
    A. A person determined by a court to be the father of the child
    B. The great-aunt of the child
    C. The doctor, midwife, or other person who delivered the child
    D. The maternal grandfather of the child

    17._____

18. Grounds for divorce in New York include all of the following EXCEPT`
    A. Cruel and inhuman treatment of the plaintiff by the defendant
    B. Abandonment of the plaintiff for a period of one or more years
    C. Confinement of the defendant in prison for a period of three or more consecutive years after the marriage of the plaintiff and defendant
    D. The dissolution of the common law marriage between the plaintiff and defendant

    18._____

Questions 19-20.

DIRECTIONS: Questions 19 and 20 are to be answered on the basis of the following information.

Amanda wants to file for divorce from Todd on the grounds of adultery. Todd carried on an affair with Amanda's co-worker, Rebecca, nearly six years ago. When Amanda discovered the affair six years ago, she immediately moved out.

19. Will Amanda's petition for divorce be granted?
    A. Yes, because adultery is a ground for divorce in the State of New York.
    B. No, because the affair was forgiven.
    C. No, because Amanda allowed Todd to have an affair and implicitly forgave him by living with him at the time the affair began.
    D. No, because Amanda's petition for divorce was not commenced within five years after the discovery of the affair.

    19._____

20. Does Amanda have the right to a trial by jury on the issues concerning the grounds for granting her divorce from Todd?
    A. No, because the adulterous affair is settled as fact
    B. No, because the affair is presumed to have ended and/or become immaterial once the divorce petition is filed
    C. No, because there is no right to a trial by jury for divorce cases
    D. Yes, because there is a right to trial by jury of the issues of the grounds for divorce.

    20._____

21. According to the New York Criminal Procedure Law, the prosecution of a petty offense must be commenced within _____ year(s).
    A. one   B. two   C. three   D. four

    21._____

22. According to the New York Criminal Procedure Law, the prosecution for a misdemeanor must be commenced within _____ year(s).
    A. one   B. two   C. three   D. four

    22._____

23. Joel, the treasurer for ABC Limited, Inc., has been stealing from the company for approximately three years. The CEO of ABC Limited, Billy, discovered the larceny nearly two years ago. Billy fired Joel but never brought charges for the theft.
Will Billy be able to prosecute Joel for larceny?
    A. Yes, because prosecution for larceny committed by a person in violation of a fiduciary duty may be commenced within three years
    B. Yes, because prosecution for larceny committed by a person in violation of a fiduciary duty may be commenced within two years
    C. No, because prosecution for larceny committed by a person in violation of a fiduciary duty must commence within one year
    D. No.

23.____

24. After a criminal action is commenced, the defendant is entitled to a _____ trial.
    A. deliberate   B. quick   C. thorough   D. speedy

24.____

25. Must the court furnish a defendant with a copy of the felony complaint during arraignment?
    A. No, because a court may furnish this information but is not required to
    B. No, because a court must furnish the complaint before trial but not at arraignment
    C. No, because the court must determine whether the defendant is to be held for grand jury
    E. Yes

25.____

KEY (CORRECT ANSWERS)

1.	D	11.	B
2.	C	12.	A
3.	D	13.	C
4.	C	14.	C
5.	B	15.	A
6.	D	16.	D
7.	C	17.	A
8.	A	18.	D
9.	C	19.	D
10.	D	20.	D

21. A
22. B
23. D
24. D
25. D

TEST 3

DIRECTIONS: Each question or incomplete statement is followed by several suggested answers or completions. Select the one that BEST answers the question or completes the statement. *PRINT THE LETTER OF THE CORRECT ANSWER IN THE SPACE AT THE RIGHT.*

1. Aggravated criminal contempt, aggravated family offense, and absconding from a community treatment facility are classified as
    A. E Felonies
    B. Violent Felonies
    C. Misdemeanors
    D. Felonies

    1._____

2. Aggravated harassment in the second degree and arson in the fifth degree are examples of
    A. Felonies
    B. Misdemeanors
    C. A Misdemeanors
    D. Violent Felonies

    2._____

3. Murder in the first degree will always be classified as a(n)
    A. Misdemeanor
    B. E Felony
    C. Felony
    D. Minor Felony

    3._____

4. A "child born out of wedlock" is
    A. any child of marriage unless dissolved
    B. any children born after the parents are married
    C. a child born after the marriage license is obtained, but before the parents are legally married
    D. any children born between two consenting adults

    4._____

5. The social welfare law maintains that in the case of neglect or inability of the parents to provide for the support and education of the child, the child is supported by the
    A. next closest kin to the mother
    B. next closest kin to the father
    C. child welfare agency of the state
    D. county, city, or town chargeable under the provision of the social welfare law

    5._____

6. The district attorney who conducts a hearing upon a felony complaint represents, or hears, the case on behalf of the
    A. county   B. city   C. people   D. government

    6._____

7. If after a hearing on a felony complaint there is a reasonable cause to believe that a defendant committed an offense that was not a felony, the court may
    A. reduce the charge but keep the felony charge on record
    B. keep the felony charge on record until the defendant is proven innocent of the lesser crime
    C. reduce the charge to one for such non-felony offense
    D. release the defendant on his or her own recognizance

    7._____

8. May a court order the removal of an action that begins in criminal court to family court?
    A. Yes, but only if the court states on record the factors upon which the determination is based
    B. Yes, but only if there are two related parties at issue
    C. Yes, but only if the complaining party consents to such a removal
    D. Yes, but only justice is better served if the case were removed to family court

9. Proceedings to establish paternity may be originated in which court? The court in the
    A. county where the mother or child resides or in the county where the putative father resides or is found
    B. city where the birth father lives
    C. county where the mother lives
    D. county where the mother birthed the child

10. If a juvenile offender defendant waives a hearing upon a felony complaint, the court must order that the defendant be held for
    A. the action of the grand jury
    B. capacity hearings
    C. guardianship determination
    D. the results of paternity

11. Bail is defined as
    A. cash or deposit
    B. deposit or bail
    C. cash or bail
    D. bail or cash

12. For the purposes recognzance, bail and commitment, an "obliger" is MOST appropriately defined as the
    A. defendant
    B. person who executes the bail bond on behalf of the defendant, assuming the undertaking
    C. co-defendant
    D. person who signs a contract indicating that they intend to post bail bond in the future

13. An appearance bond is a bail bond in which the only obligor is the
    A. defendant or principal
    B. property secured therewith
    C. defendant's co-conspirators, if any
    D. contract of appearance of the defendant

Questions 14-15.

DIRECTIONS: Questions 14 and 15 are to be answered on the basis of the following information.

Ed's mother has posted bail in the amount of $250,000 for Ed's release after he was charged with aggravated assault. The court imposed the condition that Ed appear for subsequent hearings related to the charges. Ed failed to appear for the second hearing before Judge O'Connor, who then issued a warrant for his arrest. Ed claimed his mother became gravely ill which is why he did not appear for his hearing.

14. What is the effect of Ed's failure to appear on the bail previously posted? The bail is
    A. unequivocally forfeited.
    B. generally forfeited, unless the court finds Ed had sufficient excuse for missing his appearance.
    C. reduced given the nature of Ed's mother's health condition.
    D. forfeited unless Ed's mother can produce a doctor's note.

14.____

15. Assume that the bail has been forfeited. The local criminal must pay the forfeited bail to the
    A. local village justice
    B. treasurer or other financial officer if it is a city court or the state comptroller if it is a town or village court
    C. chief justice directly
    D. treasurer of the junior congressional member of the State of New York

15.____

16. What does Leandra's Law prohibit?
    A. Driving while intoxicated with a person less than 15 years of age as a passenger in the vehicle
    B. Driving while under the influence of alcohol with other passengers in the vehicle
    C. Driving while under the influence of drugs or alcohol with a passenger less than 12 years of age in the vehicle
    D. Driving while intoxicated

16.____

17. An elderly gentleman, Dave, was assaulted at his 70th birthday celebration by another elderly man, Frank, who is ten years younger than Dave. Dave suffered various minor injuries.
    What is the MOST appropriate charge against Frank?
    A. Assault 3   B. Assault 2
    C. Harassment   D. Violent misdemeanor

17.____

18. According to the New York Civil Practice Law and Rules, when a defendant has failed to appear, plead, or proceed to trial of an action, what is the MOST appropriate remedy for a plaintiff?
    A. Resume judgment   B. Dismissal action
    C. Default judgment   D. Increase in charge

18.____

19. The party responsible for adopting rules of the courts including the preparation and publication of court calendars of the unified court system is the
    A. chief justice of the Civil Courts
    B. chief administrator of the courts
    C. comptroller of the currency
    D. bailiff of the unified court system

20. Katie sues Terry for breach of contract after Terry failed to appear for Katie's baby shower and deliver food as the contracted caterer. Terry filed a cross-claim against Samuel, whom she hired to drive her to the venue of Katie's shower. Terry alleges that because Samuel never picked her up as agreed upon, she failed to perform the catering contract for Katie.
    The action to join the claims is also known as
    A. correction of claims
    B. severance of claims
    C. joinder of claims
    D. class action

21. Generally, when actions involving a common question of law or fact are pending before the court, the court may order the actions be _____ to avoid unnecessary costs or delay.
    A. combined
    B. categorized
    C. classified
    D. consolidated

22. Justice O'Connor has ordered that certain claims in an action before the court be heard separately, or severed, from one another.
    Who is now responsible for determining the order of when each of the newly severed claims are heard?
    A. The chief justice, if not Justice O'Connor
    B. The constable
    C. The court
    D. The attorneys of record

23. Which of the following is a prerequisite to the filing of a class action?
    A. The class is so numerous that joinder of all members is impracticable.
    B. The attorneys for each class member approves the joinder of the class.
    C. Less than 500 persons embody the entire class.
    D. The class acts as a whole and accept the settlement paid as a lump sum.

24. The order permitting a class action shall do which of the following?
    A. Describe the class
    B. Set out the demand for the class
    C. Name the attorneys of record
    D. Detail the action generally

25. A class action cannot be dismissed, discontinued, or compromised without the
    A. consent of the attorneys of record
    B. approval of the court
    C. approval of the class
    D. approval of the court after a full hearing on the merits of the defense

KEY (CORRECT ANSWERS)

1.	D	11.	C
2.	B	12.	B
3.	C	13.	A
4.	B	14.	B
5.	D	15.	B
6.	C	16.	A
7.	C	17.	B
8.	A	18.	C
9.	A	19.	B
10.	A	20.	C

21. D
22. C
23. A
24. A
25. B

TEST 4

DIRECTIONS: Each question or incomplete statement is followed by several suggested answers or completions. Select the one that BEST answers the question or completes the statement. *PRINT THE LETTER OF THE CORRECT ANSWER IN THE SPACE AT THE RIGHT.*

1. During a criminal trial, where an error or other legal defect in the proceedings occurs that prejudices the defendant, the court must declare a _____ upon motion of the defendant.
   A. hung jury
   B. recantation
   C. mistrial
   D. error of motion

   1.____

2. Which party can file a motion for mistrial if it is physically impossible to proceed with the trial in conformity with the law?
   A. Defendant
   B. Plaintiff
   C. The court
   D. All of the above

   2.____

3. After issuing a trial order of dismissal which has the effect of dismissing the entire indictment, the court does which of the following immediately?
   A. Discharge the defendant from custody or exonerate the bail.
   B. Notify the defendant's next of kin
   C. Notify the complaining witness and/or victim of the dismissal
   D. Arrange for a possible appeal from the plaintiff and/or the people

   3.____

4. Generally, when the court has imposed a sentence of imprisonment, when is the last time the sentence can be changed, suspended, or interrupted?
   A. Before the sentence has commenced
   B. After the sentence has been served
   C. After the arraignment, but before the conclusion of the trial
   D. After the instructions on the charge(s) are read to the jury

   4.____

5. Judge Smith rendered a verdict in a criminal case in Essex County. However, the court did not have jurisdiction over the case. The PROPER remedy is
   A. dismissal
   B. hung jury
   C. mistrial
   D. vacate judgment

   5.____

6. The court may vacate a judgment, upon motion of the defendant, for which of the following grounds?
   A. The judgment was procured by duress.
   B. The material evidence at trial was true, but presented in a way that painted the defendant in a negative light.
   C. Material evidence was obtained for trial via search warrant or other lawful device.
   D. All of the above

   6.____

7. Rachel, a licensed eighth grade teacher, was recently convicted of felony larceny. Who must be notified of Rachel's felony conviction?
   A. Rachel's next of kin
   B. The New York Comptroller, who must garnish Rachel's pay
   C. The Department of Education
   D. The Parole Board of New York

8. Jamal knowingly filed a false financing statement for his contractor business, indicating that he owes more money than he actually does to his bank lender. Jamal was convicted of intentionally filing a false financing statement under the Uniform Commercial Code (UCC).
   Who must be notified of Jamal's conviction?
   A. The Office of the UCC
   B. The New York Secretary of State
   C. The Chief Justice
   D. The Parole Board of New York

9. During jury selection, Dawn's lawyer did not object to any potential jurors. Once the trial began, Dawn's attorney raised the objection that juror number 3, Richard, may be biased against Dawn.
   What is the MOST appropriate response to Dawn's attorney's objection?
   A. A challenge to the jury panel must be made before the selection of the jury commences, therefore overruled
   B. A challenge to the jury panel must be made before the selection of the jury ends, therefore overruled
   C. A challenge to the jury panel must be made before the selection of the jury commences, therefore accepted
   D. Sustained

10. A criminal trial jury consists of not less than _____ members.
    A. fourteen B. nine C. six D. twelve

11. Pursuant to Article 270 of the New York Criminal Procedure Law, either party may examine prospective jurors regarding their qualifications to serve as jurors. However, the court cannot allow the questioning to
    A. become repetitious, irrelevant, or involve questioning of a juror's knowledge of the rules of law
    B. reduce to questioning of the individual's family history or other background
    C. involve asking the prospective juror about his prior service on a jury
    D. contain questions that are relevant to the case, but asked in a rude or belittling manner

12. How many peremptory challenges may either side exercise during jury selection?
    A. One
    B. Two
    C. Three
    D. Dependent on the type of case

13. A challenge for cause of a prospective juror which is not made before he is sworn as a trial juror shall be deemed to be
    A. accepted   B. rebuked   C. waived   D. refuted

14. According to Section 270.16 of the New York Criminal Procedure Law, the examination of prospective jurors by either party is permitted to take place outside the presence of other prospective jurors for which type of case?
    A. Matrimonial cases, involving the adoption of a stepchild or adopted child
    B. Surrogates cases, involving complicated estates
    C. Capital cases, in which the crime charged may be punishable by death
    D. All such cases as long as the defense moves first

15. A peremptory challenge is defined as a(n)
    A. objection to a prospective juror for which no reason need be assigned
    B. objection to a prospective juror for which there must be a reason assigned
    C. objection to a prospective juror for justified cause
    D. trial objection

16. At what point in a trial is the jury provided with general instructions concerning its basic functions, duties, and conduct?
    After the jury has been sworn _____ opening address.
    A. but before the people's   B. and after the people's
    C. but before the defense's   D. and after the defense's

17. Pursuant to Section 270.45 of the New York Criminal Procedure Law, the court may in its discretion either permit a jury to _____ during recesses and/or adjournments or direct that they be continuously kept together during such periods under the supervision of an appropriate public servant.
    A. not communicate with one another
    B. not make eye contact with one another
    C. refrain from using their mobile phones
    D. separate

18. If a defendant pleads not responsible by reason of mental disease or defect, the court will ask him or her which of the following?
    A. About the offense or offenses charged in the indictment
    B. Family background
    C. Feelings or mental state at the time of the hearing
    D. Additional information not previously asked by counsel

19. Assuming the same facts as Question 18, by answering the questions posed by the court, the defendant has effectively
    A. lost his right to appeal by waiver
    B. waived his or her right to not be compelled to incriminate him or herself
    C. harmed him or herself
    D. waived his or her rights under the Second Amendment

20. Before accepting a plea of not responsible by reason of mental disease or defect, the court must find and state which of the following on record in detail?
    A. That the affirmative defense of lack of criminal responsibility by reason of mental disease or defect would be proven by the defendant at trial by a preponderance of the evidence
    B. That the defendant entered the plea under duress
    C. That the court is satisfied the defendant has been diagnosed with a generally accepted mental disease
    D. That the defendant can speak for himself

21. Intermittent imprisonment is defined as
    A. revocable sentence of imprisonment to be served on days or during certain periods of days, or both, specified by the court
    B. irrevocable sentence of imprisonment to be served part time
    C. revocable sentence of imprisonment to be served on weekends only
    D. another form of irrevocable release based on one's own recognizance

22. If John is currently serving an intermittent sentence of imprisonment and is then sentenced to a definite sentence of three years, when will he begin his definite sentence?
    A. After the conclusion of his intermittent sentence
    B. After a hearing of the court to determine which sentence takes priority
    C. After thirty days
    D. Immediately

23. Burglary in the first, second, and third degree is classified as a
    A. misdemeanor   B. minor infraction
    C. felony   D. subordinate crime

24. The crime of conspiracy is
    A. always classified as a felony
    B. always classified as a misdemeanor
    C. sometimes classified as a felony, but in other instances classified as a misdemeanor
    D. not a crime

25. The criminal sale of a firearm is
    A. always classified as a felony
    B. always classified as a violent felony
    C. sometimes classified as a felony, but in other instances classified as a misdemeanor
    D. not a crime if there is no buyer

KEY (CORRECT ANSWERS)

1.	C	11.	A
2.	D	12.	D
3.	A	13.	C
4.	A	14.	C
5.	D	15.	A
6.	A	16.	A
7.	C	17.	D
8.	B	18.	A
9.	A	19.	B
10.	D	20.	A

21. A
22. D
23. C
24. C
25. D

EXAMINATION SECTION

TEST 1

DIRECTIONS: Each question or incomplete statement is followed by several suggested answers or completions. Select the one that BEST answers the question or completes the statement. *PRINT THE LETTER OF THE CORRECT ANSWER IN THE SPACE AT THE RIGHT.*

Questions 1-3.

DIRECTIONS: Questions 1 through 3 are to be answered on the basis of the following passage.

Jim and Ace are selected to serve on a murder trial jury. Jim is asked to be excused from the jury, which is denied by the court. An alternate juror, Sarah, is selected to be added to the jury because of one of the jurors' bias against the defendant, returning the jury box to a complete panel.

1. How many jurors are currently serving? 1.____
   A. 5 B. 10 C. 12 D. 20

2. Which juror completed voir dire? 2.____
   A. Jim and Ace
   B. Ace and Sarah
   C. Jim, Ace, and Sarah
   D. None of the above

3. Which party denied Ace's request for excusal? 3.____
   A. The prosecutor
   B. The defendant's attorney
   C. The trial judge
   D. The bailiff

Questions 4-7.

DIRECTIONS: Questions 4 through 7 are to be answered on the basis of the following passage.

Josh's father, Tom, recently passed away. Josh and his sister, Rebecca, both live in Utica County. Tom lived in Richmond County. Unknowingly to Josh, in the codicil to Tom's will, he left his home to Rebecca which she disclaimed. In Surrogates Court, Josh asks the clerk for assistance in opening an estate given that his father died intestate.

4. Did Tom die intestate? 4.____
   A. Yes, because he left his home to Rebecca.
   B. Yes, because Tom was not aware of his will.
   C. Yes, because Josh formerly opened an estate in Surrogates Court.
   D. No, because Tom had a will.

5. Which party received Tom's house? 5._____
   A. Rebecca   B. Josh
   C. The administrator of the estate   D. Tom's estate

6. How many wills did Tom have? 6._____
   A. 1   B. 2   C. 3   D. 4

7. A codicil serves which of the following purpose(s)? 7._____
   A. An addition to a will that explains, revokes, or modifies the will
   B. A will replacement
   C. A real estate deed that is supplanted to the will
   D. A document that enables executors of the estate to act on the decedent's behalf

Questions 8-10.

DIRECTIONS: Questions 8 through 10 are to be answered on the basis of the following passage.

Jill and Marie were at the local McDonalds last Friday night when a man came in and held a gun to the cashier, robbing the restaurant of more than $500. When the police arrive, Jill and Marie give detailed accounts of the robbery and provide enough details for police to arrest a suspect, Donald. At arraignment, Donald pleads not guilty to armed robbery.

8. If Donald is arrested on Saturday night, when is the earliest he will be arraigned? 8._____
   A. Monday morning   B. One week later
   C. Two weeks later   D. No later than a month later

9. Which of the following will attend Donald's arraignment on his behalf? 9._____
   A. Jill and Marie   B. Marie only
   C. Donald, Donald's attorney, and Jill   D. Donald and Donald's attorney

10. Jill and Marie are _____ to Donald. 10._____
    A. eyewitnesses to a crime Donald may have committed
    B. alibis to a crime Donald may have committed
    C. markers to a crime Donald may have committed
    D. adjunct to a crime Donald likely committed

Questions 11-14.

DIRECTIONS: Questions 11 through 14 are to be answered on the basis of the following passage.

Elizabeth and Jeff recently finalized their divorce. Approximately three weeks later, Jeff has petitioned the court to pay less child support. Jeff claims that he changed jobs and can no longer afford the child support payments. In turn, Jeff stops paying child support to spite Elizabeth. Jeff is quickly arrested.

11. Jeff is in
    A. attachment
    B. garnishment
    C. arrears
    D. arraignment

12. Jeff is asking the court to approve a(n)
    A. affidavit of support
    B. order to show cause
    C. petition for withdrawal
    D. downward modification

13. Which of the following is the main element of the passage?
    A. Child support   B. Alimony   C. Paternity   D. Custody

14. Which of the following can be presumed based on the passage?
    A. Jeff and Elizabeth have at least one child together
    B. Jeff and Elizabeth are divorced
    C. Jeff and Elizabeth are employed
    D. All of the above

Questions 15-16.

DIRECTIONS: Questions 15 and 16 are to be answered on the basis of the following passage.

At a bond review, Jason's attorney asks that the amount of the bond be reduced from $1 million to $250,000. The court asks for justification for the request and hears arguments from both sides.

15. Which of the following can be inferred about Jason?
    A. Jason is an adult.
    B. Jason was arrested for a crime.
    C. Jason lives by himself.
    D. Jason is a convicted felon.

16. Which type of bond is Jason required to pay?
    A. Promise to appear
    B. Appellate bond
    C. Surety bond
    D. Capital bond

Questions 17-20.

DIRECTIONS: Questions 17 through 20 are to be answered on the basis of the following passage.

Attorneys for Orange Bank and Grape Bank have asked the court for three different continuances. The Court asked the attorneys to agree on a number of matters, including discovery requests, and to consider settling. The attorneys ask for one more continuance and set a date three months away.

17. During which of the following will the judge encourage stipulations?
    A. Pre-trial conference
    B. Arraignment
    C. Settlement
    D. Entry of arbitration

18. The continuance date is the date
    A. in which the next hearing will be held in court
    B. attorneys agree to settle
    C. the trial will begin
    D. the trial will end

19. Which of the following are recorded in the docket?
    A. The last agreed upon hearing
    B. The first three hearings only
    C. The final trial date only
    D. All court hearings

20. Assuming the case is taking place in New York City, the current case is MOST likely being tried in which of the following?
    A. Kings County Criminal Court
    B. Richmond County Criminal Court
    C. New York City Civil Court
    D. Surrogates Court

Questions 21-25.

DIRECTIONS: Questions 21 through 25 are to be answered on the basis of the following passage.

While walking home one afternoon, Amara is struck from behind and robbed of her cell phone, smartwatch, and handbag. Amara strongly believes that one of the teenagers in the neighborhood committed the crime after seeing her attacker flee down the street. Amara files a police report and, after a few weeks, the police arrest Jane for the crime.

21. When is the first time Amara will see Jane in a courtroom setting?
    A. At Jane's trial
    B. At Jane's pre-hearing conference
    C. At Jane's arraignment
    D. At Jane's deposition

22. What can be inferred about Jane's criminal status from the above passage?
    A. One cannot assume she has a criminal past.
    B. One can assume Jane is a convicted felon.
    C. One can assume Jane is a repeat offender.
    D. One can assume Jane is guilty of the assault against Amara.

23. If Jane is tried, which of the following parties is MOST likely to serve as the attorney on Amara's behalf?
    A. Amara's chosen attorney
    B. Amara will likely represent herself
    C. Assistant District Attorney
    D. Federal Prosecutor

24. Assume that Amara is severely beaten and in critical condition after the assault. How would that affect who will legally represent Amara?
    A. The charges will be elevated to murder.
    B. The charges will decreased to the misdemeanor level.
    C. Amara's legal representation will not change.
    D. Jane will need to agree to a plea bargain to avoid jail time.

25. If Jane is sentenced to more than one year in prison, she will be guilty of a   25._____
    A. civil action   B. offense   C. felony   D. violation

KEY (CORRECT ANSWERS)

1.	C	11.	C
2.	C	12.	D
3.	C	13.	A
4.	D	14.	D
5.	D	15.	B
6.	A	16.	C
7.	A	17.	A
8.	A	18.	A
9.	D	19.	D
10.	A	20.	C

21. C
22. A
23. C
24. C
25. C

TEST 2

DIRECTIONS: Each question or incomplete statement is followed by several suggested answers or completions. Select the one that BEST answers the question or completes the statement. *PRINT THE LETTER OF THE CORRECT ANSWER IN THE SPACE AT THE RIGHT.*

Questions 1-3.

DIRECTIONS: Questions 1 through 3 are to be answered on the basis of the following passage.

The owner of a local restaurant, Bob, is suing Jason for defamation after Jason published a number of articles and posts online about Bob and Bob's restaurant. After hours of deliberation, the jury returned a verdict in Jason's favor.

1. What can be inferred from the passage about the procedure of the case? 1.____
   A. The matter was settled out of court.
   B. The parties were likely referred to arbitration.
   C. There was a trial.
   D. The parties are related.

2. Jason is which of the following in the case? 2.____
   A. Plaintiff   B. Appellant   C. Appellee   D. Respondent

3. Deliberations indicate which of the following? 3.____
   A. The jury discussed the case for some time.
   B. The jury did not discuss the case.
   C. The jury agreed with Bob.
   D. The jury could not arrive at a decision.

Questions 4-6.

DIRECTIONS: Questions 4 through 6 are to be answered on the basis of the following passage.

Sam's home is the subject of an __(4)__, which is the legal process by which real estate of a private owner is taken for public use upon the award and payment of compensation. Sam __(5)__ the amount of compensation he deserves for his home and wants to file a suit against the State of New York. Ultimately, though, the case is adjudicated in the government's __(6)__.

4. The CORRECT word to fill in space number 4 is 4.____
   A. res judicata
   B. collateral estoppel
   C. criminal mischief
   D. eminent domain

5. The CORRECT word to fill in space number 5 is 5.____
   A. disputes   B. relieves   C. argues   D. denies

6. The CORRECT word to fill in space number 6 is
   A. favor   B. side   C. repute   D. decision

Questions 7-10.

DIRECTIONS: Questions 7 through 10 are to be answered on the basis of the following passage.

At the end of a divorce proceeding, the Court orders Bill to pay Jill alimony in the amount of $350 per month. Both Bill and Jill are represented by attorneys. While there are many grounds for divorce in New York, although the divorce between Bill and Jill is uncontested.

7. Which of the following is not determined in the proceeding?
   A. Child support
   B. Child custody
   C. Visitation
   D. All of the above

8. The end result of the divorce proceeding is
   A. dissolution of marriage
   B. annulment of union
   C. approval of union petition
   D. dissolution of certificate of marriage

9. Given that Bill and Jill's divorce is uncontested, which of the following can be assumed?
   A. Bill and Jill cannot agree on financial matters and division of assets.
   B. Bill and Jill cannot agree on child custody matters.
   C. Bill and Jill's divorce hearings are adversarial.
   D. Bill and Jill agree on most finance and divorce-related issues.

10. Which of the following is MOST likely to be filed in the divorce matter?
    A. Eyewitness testimony
    B. Statement of net worth
    C. Codicil(s)
    D. Adoption documentation

Questions 11-14.

DIRECTIONS: Questions 11 through 14 are to be answered on the basis of the following passage.

Laura is a __(11)__ to the case of The People v. Jones, a criminal trial relating to the murder of Arthur Smith. The defendant on trial for the crime is Wesley Jones. Sarah's testimony has already been determined as relevant and substantial. Laura's testimony is ultimately recorded in the __(12)__ of the Court Clerk's Journal of Courtroom Proceedings.

11. The CORRECT word to fill in space number 11 is
    A. material witness
    B. insubstantial account
    C. in rem litigant
    D. testifier

12. Which of the following is MOST likely about Laura's testimony? 12.____
    A. Laura witnessed the crime.
    B. Laura knows Arthur Smith.
    C. Laura knows Wesley Jones.
    D. Laura does not know specific details of the crime.

13. The CORRECT word to fill in space number 13 is 13.____
    A. notes   B. minutes   C. projects   D. task book

14. Which of the following would Laura do before testifying? 14.____
    A. Sign an affidavit
    B. Take an oath
    C. Discharge unrelated duties
    D. Execute a notary public-signed complaint

Questions 15-17.

DIRECTIONS: Questions 15 through 17 are to be answered on the basis of the following passage.

During the pre-trial conference, the judge presiding over a civil matter notices that the venue is defective. Neither party lives in the county in which the dispute takes place and neither party seems to have noticed the defect before the case was filed.

15. Venue is important because 15.____
    A. it is the geographical place where legal matters may be decided in a case
    B. the outcome of the case is determined based on venue
    C. the parties live in close proximity to the courthouse
    D. venue determines the applicable law

16. A defect in venue can be 16.____
    A. ignored by the judge   B. waived by the judge
    C. waived by the parties   D. ignored by the parties

17. Venue is often confused with _____, which is the place in which a person has 17.____
    a true and permanent home.
    A. jurisdiction   B. domicile   C. residence   D. permanence

Questions 18-21.

DIRECTIONS: Questions 18 through 21 are to be answered on the basis of the following passage.

There are numerous people in the courtroom during a trial inclusive of the parties, judge, jury, attorneys, and court clerks. Other personnel that may be involved in a trial are __(18)__ or __(18)__ who testify and __(19)__ who may be necessary if any of the parties require a translator.

18. The CORRECT words to fill in space numbers 18 are
    A. witnesses; experts
    B. personnel; experts
    C. alternatives; witnesses
    D. alternates; experts

19. The CORRECT word to fill in space number 19 is
    A. interpreters
    B. speakers
    C. assistants
    D. affiants

20. Which of the following parties are sequestered to ensure a fair and impartial trial process?
    A. Attorneys
    B. Parties
    C. Jurors
    D. Clerk

21. Which party will likely be part of the entire trial?
    A. Jurors
    B. Parties
    C. Clerks
    D. All of the above

Questions 22-25.

DIRECTIONS: Questions 22 through 25 are to be answered on the basis of the following passage.

Earl hired an attorney to file a lawsuit against his former employer, Gates Law, PLLC, a law firm in Bronx County for breach of contract relating to his time as an attorney for the firm. Although Judge Smith is scheduled to preside over the case, she has to recuse herself as she used to work for Gates Law, PLLC, which is particularly important since Earl's attorney has requested a bench trial.

22. The judge has done which of the following?
    A. Recused herself
    B. Redacted herself
    C. Impartially excused herself
    D. Excused herself

23. Which of the following is the cause of action in the case?
    A. Unlawful firing
    B. Withholding of pay
    C. Discriminatory action
    D. Breach of contract

24. The cause of action in this matter classifies this case as a(n)
    A. infraction
    B. civil matter
    C. criminal matter
    D. family court matter

25. Which of the following parties MOST likely resides in Bronx County?
    A. The judge
    B. The majority of the jury
    C. Earl
    D. One current employee of Gates Law, PLLC

KEY (CORRECT ANSWERS)

1.	C	11.	A
2.	D	12.	A
3.	A	13.	B
4.	D	14.	B
5.	A	15.	A
6.	A	16.	C
7.	D	17.	B
8.	A	18.	A
9.	D	19.	A
10.	B	20.	C

21. D
22. A
23. D
24. C
25. C

EXAMINATION SECTION

TEST 1

DIRECTIONS: Each question or incomplete statement is followed by several suggested answers or completions. Select the one that BEST answers the question or completes the statement. *PRINT THE LETTER OF THE CORRECT ANSWER IN THE SPACE AT THE RIGHT.*

Questions 1-5.

DIRECTIONS: Questions 1 through 5 are to be answered on the basis of the following fact pattern.

When Family Court opens on Monday morning, Desiree rushes to the clerk's desk in a panic. Her ex-boyfriend, Alex, has made threats against her and her children and she would like to file a restraining order as soon as possible. She has never been in court before and does not have any idea of what to expect or what she may need, but she is in fear of her and her children's lives.

1. While Desiree fears for her safety, she cannot obtain a final order of protection against Alex. Why?
    A. A judge has not yet been assigned to the case.
    B. A judge has not been assigned, so there has been no finding of a family offense being committed and Alex has not agreed to the order.
    C. Desiree's children should be present for the request to the court unless they are under age 18.
    D. Alex has not agreed to the order.

2. A temporary restraining order only lasts until
    A. the close of the case
    B. the beginning of an appeal
    C. the next time the petitioner is in court
    D. it is extended indefinitely

3. Desiree asks how long a final order of protection lasts. The MOST appropriate response is
    A. two or ten years
    B. two or five years
    C. one year
    D. six months

4. Which party is responsible for drafting the petition to the judge for a temporary restraining order?
    A. The judge
    B. The party seeking the order
    C. The clerk
    D. A spectator

5. After Desiree starts her case, Alex is served with a summons. Three weeks later, Desiree returns to the courthouse to say that she has changed her mind and no longer fears for her safety.
Desiree must
   A. withdraw her petition for a restraining order
   B. start an anger management program
   C. withdraw her petition with prejudice as she will not be able to file again
   D. recuse herself

6. Jamie has hired legal counsel to represent him in the purchase of commercial buildings across New York State. With his attorney's help, he has secured the purchase of nine different office buildings totaling $2 million. Last week, Jamie discovered that his attorney forged his signature on the sale of four of those properties and collected the proceeds. Assume the threshold for filing a suit in Albany County is $50,000, Nassau County is $200,000, and New York County is $500,000.
Where can Jamie sue his attorney for malpractice?
   A. New York County
   B. Albany County
   C. Nassau County
   D. All of the above

7. Which of the following matters is LEAST likely to be heard in the Albany County – Commercial Division?
   A. Commercial class actions
   B. Transactions governed by the Uniform Commercial Code
   C. Divorce
   D. Shareholder derivate action

8. Which of the following matters is LEAST likely to be heard in Suffolk County District Court?
   A. Small claims matter of $1,000,000
   B. Arraignment in a felony case
   C. Petty larceny (theft of $200)
   D. Shoplifting

9. Which of the following is LEAST likely to be heard in the Landlord and Tenant Court?
   A. Non-payment proceedings
   B. Hold-over proceedings
   C. Evictions
   D. Adoptions

10. Dave approaches the clerk's desk and insists that he has a tenant in his building who refuses to pay rent and will not vacate the premises.
Dave seeks assistance on initiating _____ proceedings.
   A. Annulment   B. Hold-over   C. Numeration   D. Abandonment

11. John and Jill need to file for bankruptcy and would like to do so together.
John and Jill would file which type of petition?
   A. Separate   B. Tenants   C. Survivor   D. Joint

12. Rich would like to know what advice he can give his brother who was arrested last night for driving under the influence of alcohol. Rich's brother is scheduled to be arraigned this morning. While you may not be authorized to give legal advice, it is prudent to know that a plea of nolo contendere has the same effect as a plea of _____, but is not an admission of guilt.
    A. acquittal   B. remorse   C. not guilty   D. guilty

    12._____

13. Emily arrives in court for her bankruptcy hearing. Emily is not working, does not have any savings. She does not own any property, jewelry, collectibles, or other precious items of value.
    Emily's bankruptcy petition will MOST likely be classified as a _____ case.
    A. nolo contendere   B. no asset
    C. no prohibition   D. Chapter 13

    13._____

14. Assume the same facts as above. Emily is a full-time student and took out a student loan before filing bankruptcy.
    The trustee has informed Emily her student loan is a _____ debt.
    A. dischargeable   B. non-dischargeable
    C. immediate   D. short term

    14._____

15. A party in interest in bankruptcy is defined as a party who
    A. has standing to be heard in a matter to be decided in the bankruptcy case
    B. standing to disrupt the court
    C. intends to file a brief
    D. intends to petition for early release

    15._____

16. A petty offense is one that is punishable by _____ or less in prison.
    A. six months   B. one year   C. three years   D. four years

    16._____

17. Town and village courts have jurisdiction over
    A. vehicle and traffic matters   B. small claims
    C. civil matters   D. all of the above

    17._____

18. The highest civil court in New York is the
    A. Supreme Court   B. City Court
    C. Civil Court   D. Court of Appeals

    18._____

19. The highest criminal court in New York is the
    A. New York City Criminal Court   B. Court of Appeals
    C. County Courts   D. Village Courts

    19._____

Questions 20-23.

DIRECTIONS: Questions 20 through 23 are to be answered on the basis of the following fact pattern.

Amy is a Guardians ad Litem ("GAL") for the New York Housing Court. She volunteered for the Court because she wanted to help people resolve their housing disputes. The judge has appointed Amy as Gerald's GAL in his case. Gerald is involved in a minor dispute with his landlord.

20. Amy believes that Gerald's housing issues stem from his poor money management. Can Amy manage Gerald's checkbook and other personal finances as they relate to his housing case?
    A. Yes, because his finances relate to his housing case
    B. Yes, because he clearly cannot manage his money on his own
    C. Yes, but only if Gerald asks her to
    D. No

21. Amy is NOT allowed to do which of the following things?
    A. Meet with Gerald
    B. Meet with Gerald's landlord
    C. Allow Gerald's landlord into Gerald's apartment
    D. Ensure the landlord completes repairs as promised

22. A GAL works in which party's best interest?
    A. Gerald's landlord   B. Gerald
    C. The appointed party   D. The judge

23. Amy has fallen ill and cannot meet her obligations as a GAL. Which party can remove Amy as Gerald's GAL?
    A. Gerald   B. Gerald's landlord
    C. The judge   D. The clerk

24. Pro per is another term for _____ or a self-represented person.
    A. pro tem   B. pro se   C. qui tam   D. quid pro

25. Sanctions are defined as a
    A. penalty or other type of enforcement used to bring about compliance with the law
    B. penalty specific to international trade law
    C. federal penalty reserved for those who lie under oath
    D. misdemeanor crime punishable by more than four years in prison

KEY (CORRECT ANSWERS)

1.	A		11.	D
2.	C		12.	D
3.	B		13.	B
4.	C		14.	B
5.	A		15.	A
6.	D		16.	A
7.	C		17.	D
8.	A		18.	D
9.	D		19.	B
10.	B		20.	D

21. C
22. C
23. C
24. B
25. A

TEST 2

DIRECTIONS: Each question or incomplete statement is followed by several suggested answers or completions. Select the one that BEST answers the question or completes the statement. *PRINT THE LETTER OF THE CORRECT ANSWER IN THE SPACE AT THE RIGHT.*

Questions 1-5.

DIRECTIONS: Questions 1 through 5 are to be answered on the basis of the following fact pattern.

Edwin has been served with a lawsuit from his former accountant, Bob. Bob claims Edwin never paid him for his accounting services after he filed Edwin's personal income tax and business income tax returns. Edwin has come to the clerk's desk confused and angry.

1. Edwin wants to know what the basis of Bob's legal claim is against him. Where can Edwin find more information about the case?
   A. The internet
   B. The complaint
   C. The subpoena
   D. The arraignment

2. Edwin claims that he was audited by the IRS shortly after Bob filed his personal income taxes. Edwin wants to sue Bob in connection with his being audited. In order to do so, Edwin would need to
   A. re-sue
   B. re-file
   C. countersue
   D. cross-claim

3. Bob filed taxes for Edwin and Edwin's wife. While Edwin's wife is not listed on the Complaint in Edwin's suit against Bob, Edwin's wife would also like to appear as a party to the case. Is this possible?
   A. No, because Edwin's wife may be unavailable for trial
   B. No, because Edwin's wife is not initiating the suit
   C. No, because Edwin can only sue Bob himself
   D. Yes

4. Which of the following courts is MOST appropriate for Edwin's suit against Bob?
   A. Housing Court
   B. Surrogates Court
   C. Civil Court
   D. Criminal Court

5. Which of the following is MOST likely to be the legal basis of Bob's suit against Edwin?
   A. Breach of contract
   B. Negligence
   C. Assault
   D. Defamation

1.____
2.____
3.____
4.____
5.____

6. The Housing Court is made of parts. The resolution part presides over all pre-trial matters in a case and attempts to settle the case. Jeremy appears at Housing Court for his trial that begins this morning.
Is Jeremy's case appropriate for the pre-trial part of the Housing Court?
   A. Yes, as pre-trial matters preclude this
   B. Yes, as a check in before the trial can start
   C. No, the trial part is separate and distinct from the pre-trial part of Housing Court
   D. No, the trial part only hears cases on Mondays

6.____

Questions 7-8.

DIRECTIONS: Questions 7 and 8 are to be answered on the basis of the following text.

Jenny received a notice from the marshal that she is being evicted from her apartment. She wants to ignore the notice, but comes to the courthouse at the urging of her boyfriend.

7. Her boyfriend warns her that if she does not take care of the notice, she and her _____ may be _____ from the apartment.
   A. property; removed
   B. removed; property
   C. property; removal
   D. assets; removed

7.____

8. At the courthouse, the clerk instructs Jenny to complete an affidavit in support of a(n)
   A. order for removal
   B. petition
   C. order to show cause
   D. justification

8.____

9. Because Jenny never answered the original petition for eviction from her landlord, her landlord obtained a _____ judgment against her. Jenny now needs to complete an affidavit in support of an order to show cause to _____ a judgment based on failure to answer.
   A. vacate; default
   B. vacate; demand
   C. default; vacate
   D. default; validate

9.____

10. A clerk in the Resolution Part of Housing Court can do all of the following EXCEPT
    A. answer questions about the court calendar
    B. answer questions about the judge's rules
    C. assist the judge as necessary
    D. provide detailed legal analysis and/or advice

10.____

11. A judge may direct parties in a dispute to mediation, which is a form of
    A. neutrality
    B. alternative dispute resolution
    C. alternative judgment
    D. non-binding analysis of the legal dispute

11.____

12. Joel and Rachel would like to place their daughter into foster care. 12.____
Do Joel and Rachel need an attorney to represent them in court?
    A. Yes, as foster care placements are complicated
    B. Yes, unless they do not have money to hire a lawyer
    C. No, legal representation is not required but they do have a right to have the court appoint an attorney if they cannot afford one
    D. No, unless they change their minds after the placement has taken place

13. The New York Court of Claims is the only court where one can seek damages against 13.____
    A. the State of New York or other state-related agencies
    B. New York City
    C. municipalities in Richmond County
    D. New York State colleges

14. While City Courts such as Binghamton City Court handle criminal and civil matters, the amount in dispute can only be up to 14.____
    A. $20,000,000   B. $15,000   C. $1,000,000   D. $5,000,000

15. Beatrice is having issues understanding her mother's will. Her mother is living, but Beatrice wants to ensure she understands all of the terms of the will while her mother is still alive. 15.____
Beatrice is not the named executor, which is defined as
    A. someone named in the will appointed to wind up the affairs of the deceased person
    B. the person who inherits all of the deceased person's property
    C. the attorney of the estate
    D. the judge who presides over the estate

16. A person who is named in the will to inherit money or other property is the 16.____
    A. executrix   B. devisee   C. custodian   D. beneficiary

17. Matters of will and probate are heard in which court? 17.____
    A. Civil Court   B. Family Court
    C. Surrogates Court   D. Criminal Court

18. A revocable trust is a trust that can be 18.____
    A. rescinded by the grantor after creation
    B. overruled by a judge
    C. nullified by the beneficiaries
    D. canceled outright without warning to the trust remainders

19. James approaches the clerk's desk seeking assistance regarding a child support matter. James lost his job a few months ago and can no longer pay his child support. 19.____
What is the LEAST appropriate advice you can give James?
    A. He is prudent for coming to the court to seek assistance as there are serious penalties for non-payment of child support.
    B. A support order can be modified.

C. Without income, he cannot possibly pay child support, so he should wait until he is found in contempt of court.
D. Penalties for non-payment include interception of tax refunds, suspension of personal and business licenses, and seizure of bank accounts.

20. As a clerk for the New York Court of Appeals, you are asked to determine whether a case from one of the trial courts has been upheld or reversed. If the case has been upheld, it is recorded in the docket as
    A. remanded   b. retained   C. affirmed   D. affiant

21. If a case has been reversed or sent back to the trial court from the New York Court of Appeals, the word _____ will be recorded in the docket.
    A. retained   B. reversed   C. remanded   D. replevin

22. Sue does not agree with the finding of the Family Court. She asks if an order can be appealed.
    The MOST appropriate response is:
    A. No, as all orders are final
    B. No, as Family Court does not pose any legal issues requiring appeal
    C. No, given that Sue is not represented by an attorney
    D. Yes, she may appeal from an order

23. Joe, John, and Beth are involved in a paternity suit. Joe believes he is the father of Beth's baby, Sarah, but John maintains that he is the father.
    What document would be MOST helpful for the court in resolving this matter?
    A. John and Beth's marriage license
    B. Joe and Beth's marriage license
    C. Sarah's birth certificate
    D. Beth's medical records

24. Abel is concerned that his cousin, Ted, is not able to afford legal representation in his trial for armed robbery. Ted must be considered _____ or otherwise unable to afford to hire a lawyer before defense counsel is appointed by the court.
    A. responsible   B. indigent   C. not guilty   D. petty

25. Which of the following is heard and determined outside of the courtroom?
    A. Hearing   B. Plea bargain
    C. Testimony   D. Evidence

KEY (CORRECT ANSWERS)

1.	B	11.	B
2.	C	12.	C
3.	D	13.	A
4.	C	14.	B
5.	A	15.	A
6.	C	16.	D
7.	A	17.	C
8.	C	18.	A
9.	C	19.	C
10.	D	20.	C

21.	C
22.	D
23.	C
24.	B
25.	B

EXAMINATION SECTION

TEST 1

DIRECTIONS: Each question or incomplete statement is followed by several suggested answers or completions. Select the one that BEST answers the question or completes the statement. *PRINT THE LETTER OF THE CORRECT ANSWER IN THE SPACE AT THE RIGHT.*

Questions 1-5.

DIRECTIONS: Questions 1 through 5 are to be answered on the basis of the following fact pattern.

Bill initiated a lawsuit against his landlord, Amy, last year. Bill claims Amy did not upkeep common areas in the four-apartment building where Bill resides. These common areas include the hallway, entryway, and parking lot of the building. Bill is not represented by an attorney, but Amy is represented by Maureen. The parties have failed to settle the matter outside of court. Bill, Amy, and Maureen are ready to move forward with court proceedings.

1. The magistrate judge sets the pre-trial conference between the parties for March 30 at 9:30 A.M. The parties required to attend the pretrial conference are
   A. Maureen, Bill, and the judge
   B. the judge only
   C. Bill and Amy
   D. Bill, Amy, and Maureen

2. During the pre-trial conference, the judge wants the parties to stipulate to as many issues as possible before trial. The judge instructs the parties to focus on undisputed facts. An example of a stipulation would be:
   A. Both parties agree the parking lot is not a common area
   B. Maureen files a motion to vacate
   C. Bill wants to expedite the case and start trial the following Monday]
   D. Amy files a counterclaim against Bill for failure to pay rent on time

3. A pre-trial conference is attended by the required parties if the case does not settle before trial. However, a pre-trial conference cannot be set until
   A. the jury is selected
   B. the attorneys have entered appearances
   C. initial pleadings, including the complaint and answer, have been filed
   D. the court clerk is selected

4. Which deadline is MOST likely to be set by the judge during the pre-trial conference?
   The deadline
   A. to decide which juror will serve as foreperson
   B. to decide which courthouse the trial will take place
   C. for all discovery to be completed
   D. for the judge to select a law clerk to transcribe court proceedings

5. Bill will be appearing as a
   A. defendant
   B. pro se litigant
   C. respondent
   D. en banc party

Questions 6-9.

DIRECTIONS: Questions 6 through 9 are to be answered on the basis of the following fact pattern.

Adam, Barbara, Cameron, and David appear for jury duty on June 15. Adam and Barbara have each served on a trial before; Adam served on a criminal trial while Barbara served on a civil trial. The trial Adam served on lasted three months, and he would prefer not to serve on a trial ever again. Cameron and David have never served on a trial before and are unsure of what to expect.

6. While prospective jurors wait to be called by the clerk, Adam and Cameron spark up a conversation. Adam tells Cameron that if he were selected to be a juror Cameron may be isolated from his family and friends for weeks.
   What is Adam referring to?
   A. Ex-parte communications, which prohibit jurors from speaking with anyone else during the trial
   B. Voir dire, which may require one to be questioned in judge's chambers about past dealings
   C. Jury sequestration or juror isolation from the public to prevent contact with outside influences
   D. Individual depositions of jurors prior to the start of a trial

7. Barbara overhears the conversation between Adam and Cameron and interjects. She explains that not all juries operate the same way. She explains that in the middle of the trial in which she served, the defendant filed a motion requesting a bench trial.
   A bench trial is a trial without a
   A. plaintiff's attorney
   B. jury
   C. defendant's attorney
   D. bailiff

8. The court's clerk finally begins jury selection. He or she calls how many jurors from the jury selection list?
   A. 9
   B. 6
   C. 10
   D. 12

9. Cameron and David are selected and take a seat in the jury box. The judge provides an overview of the case and tells the prospective jurors that the case involves armed robbery. As a teenager, David was mugged at gunpoint while walking home from school. He raises his hand and tells the judge he may be biased in the trial because of his personal experience.
   The defendant's attorney will ask that David be excused
   A. with good reason
   B. for cause
   C. without prejudice
   D. with prejudice

10. Which of the following does NOT occur during the judge's charge to the jury?
    A. A discussion of the standard of proof jurors should apply to the case
    B. A reminder that opening and closing arguments are considered evidence
    C. A note that jurors should base their conclusions on the evidence presented at trial
    D. A reminder that jurors are required to adhere to the relevant laws in rendering a verdict

11. Which of the following does the court reporter NOT record
    A. testimony of the witnesses
    B. objections made by the attorneys
    C. the judge's respective rulings of objections
    D. ex-parte communications

Questions 12-16.

DIRECTIONS: Questions 12 through 16 are to be answered on the basis of the following fact pattern.

Michael is accused of felony theft of an automobile. The vehicle was taken from an 18-unit apartment building parking lot sometime during the night of August 15. The vehicle was driven for approximately five miles before the driver crashed it into a parked car. The driver fled the scene. The owner of the vehicle, Jeffrey, was asleep in his apartment during the time the vehicle was stolen. Michael and Jeffrey are represented by counsel.

12. Given the charge of felony theft of an automobile, Michael now faces how long a term of incarceration?
    A. One year or more
    B. One year or less
    C. Six months
    D. Five years or more

13. During Jeffrey's testimony, one of the jurors, Samantha, realizes she was in the building where the car was stolen on the night of the theft. She was sleeping over her sister's apartment for the night and remembers seeing a bright blue Porsche – Jeffrey's car – in the parking lot before bed. She immediately informs the bailiff who tells the judge.
    How will the judge MOST likely move forward in the case?
    A. Declare a mistrial
    B. Acquit Michael of all charges
    C. Excuse the juror and replace here with an alternate juror and continue the trial
    D. Demand the attorneys in the case submit post-hearing briefs on the issue

14. In open court, the judge asks Samantha details about why she was in the apartment at the time Michael allegedly stole Jeffrey's car and what, if anything, she remembers about that night. Samantha says she did not see or hear anything suspicious, but does remember Michael being in the apartment building in one of the common areas. Michael's attorney files a motion for a mistrial after Samantha's testimony to the court. Why?

A. Samantha's testimony has substantially prejudiced the other jurors who heard Michael was in the building on the night of the theft.
B. There is not enough substantive evidence to continue the trial against Michael.
C. Samantha should have been removed as a juror at the beginning of the trial.
D. The case must be filed in the court closest to where the car was found, not where it was allegedly taken.

15. If the judge declares a mistrial, what effect would that determination have on the jury verdict?
    A. No effect; the jury must still render a decision on the merits
    B. The jury need only to determine damages.
    C. The jury does not need to render a verdict.
    D. Only six jurors need to serve after the judge declares a mistrial.

16. After all evidence has been presented, it is clear Michael did not commit the crime. Michael was in another state at the time of the theft and could not have committed felony theft of Jeffrey's automobile. Before the case is submitted to a jury, Michael's attorney submits a motion that argues no reasonable jury could find for Jeffrey. Michael's attorney asks the judge to instruct the jury to find Michael not guilty.
    Michael's attorney is requesting a(n) _____, because Michael clearly did not commit the crime.
    A. reduced charge
    B. substitute charge
    C. acquittal
    D. directed verdict

17. During the direct examination of one of the plaintiff's witnesses, the defendant's attorney objects. Defendant's attorney believes opposing counsel asked a leading question. The judge sustains defendant's objection.
    How must plaintiff's counsel proceed?
    A. The witness may answer the question as asked.
    B. Plaintiff's counsel must re-phrase the question in a proper form or ask another question.
    C. Plaintiff's counsel must stop his or her line of questioning completely.
    D. The witness may step down.

18. An expert is permitted to
    A. review the plaintiff's evidence, draw a reasonable conclusion, and give testimony to that effect
    B. review the defendant's evidence, draw a reasonable conclusion, and submit his or her opinion in writing to the judge
    C. give his or her opinion based on the facts in evidence and provide the reasoning for that opinion
    D. provide an opinion in open court

19. Which party, as a matter of right, is entitled to a rebuttal in closing arguments?
    A. The plaintiff
    B. The defense
    C. The defense, but only after the plaintiff has given their closing argument
    D. The defense, but only if the plaintiff waives their right to make a closing argument

20. When a jury cannot agree on a verdict, a(n) _____ occurs and the result is a(n) _____.
    A. mistrial; acquittal
    B. mistrial; hung jury
    C. hung jury; mistrial
    D. acquittal; mistrial

21. Generally speaking, the role of the foreperson, also known as the presiding juror, is to
    A. announce the verdict
    B. preside over discussion of the jurors
    C. preside over the votes of the jurors
    D. all of the above

22. A request to poll the jury serves what purpose?
    Jury polling
    A. ensures the verdict to be recorded is accurate
    B. allows jurors to resolve any conflicts of interests prior to the start of trial
    C. helps the jury selection process move faster
    D. allows the judge to ensure each juror will be impartial and unbiased while hearing evidence

23. In which of the following scenarios would a bailiff MOST likely intervene?
    A. The plaintiff and defense attorneys are chatting with one another outside the courtroom.
    B. The judge and his or her law clerk are overheard talking about the case in judge's chambers.
    C. One of the jurors is talking with the defense attorney inside the courtroom before others have entered the room.
    D. The plaintiff and the defendant's attorney are heard talking in the hallway.

24. Which of the following would be submitted only after a verdict is rendered?
    A. Motion to dismiss
    B. Motion in limine
    C. Motion to exclude
    D. Motion in arrest of judgment

25. In many jurisdictions, a motion for a new trial must be filed before a party can file a(n)
    A. exculpatory plea
    B. motion for mistrial
    C. acquittal by default
    D. appeal

KEY (CORRECT ANSWERS)

1. A
2. A
3. C
4. C
5. B

6. C
7. B
8. D
9. B
10. B

11. D
12. A
13. C
14. A
15. C

16. D
17. B
18. C
19. A
20. C

21. D
22. A
23. C
24. D
25. D

TEST 2

DIRECTIONS: Each question or incomplete statement is followed by several suggested answers or completions. Select the one that BEST answers the question or completes the statement. *PRINT THE LETTER OF THE CORRECT ANSWER IN THE SPACE AT THE RIGHT.*

Questions 1-5.

DIRECTIONS: Questions 1 through 5 are to be answered on the basis of the following fact pattern.

James and Sean started an accounting practice five years ago. Business quickly soured and James and Sean decided to each start their own competing business practices. While James' business flourished, Sean's practice has floundered. Sean believes James spoke poorly about him to their mutual friends, ruining his professional reputation, and went behind his back to steal clients. Sean now wants to sue James civilly.

1. How would Sean begin a civil suit against James?
   A. Sean needs to file an interpleader to compel James to court.
   B. Sean must file a motion to compel proceedings.
   C. Sean must file a complaint against Sean in the proper court.
   D. Sean can outline the facts of his case to the clerk who will transcribe the issues.

2. Sean must also file a summons with the clerk.
   What is the role of the summons in initiating a lawsuit?
   A. It puts the other party on notice that a lawsuit has been filed against them.
   B. It compels discovery in a court of proper jurisdiction.
   C. It requires the other party to answer by initiating a cross-motion.
   D. It gives the other party extended time to file a counterclaim.

3. Sean's attorney and James' attorney begin the process of exchanging information about the witnesses each side plans to call and the evidence that will be presented at trial.
   This process is called
   A. interrogation   B. discovery   C. compulsion   D. demurrer

4. One of James' and Sean's former clients is moving to London. James' and Sean's attorneys agree to take her deposition now and use it at trial in the event she will not be able to appear.
   At trial, her testimony will be _____ and part of the record.
   A. read into evidence   B. ex parte
   C. sequestered   D. assumed credible

5. After being notified that a lawsuit has been filed against him, James has an opportunity to answer the _____ that has been filed against him.
   A. pleadings   B. motion to compel
   C. interpleader   D. complaint

6. Venue refers to the district or county within a state where the
   A. lawsuit began
   B. lawsuit must be heard
   C. plaintiff resides
   D. plaintiff is domiciled

7. After both parties have agreed on a jury, the jurors are _____ by the court clerk before they are impaneled.
   A. instructed to take notes
   B. sworn in
   C. fingerprinted
   D. arranged

8. Can the prosecution compel a defendant in a criminal trial to take the stand and testify?
   A. Yes; he or she must explain what happened in open court
   B. Yes; he or she must take the stand and testify they are using their Fifth Amendment right against self-incrimination.
   C. Yes; he or she must take the stand but they can refuse to answer any question they choose.
   D. No.

9. Criminal charges are brought against a person in all of the following ways, EXCEPT
   A. citation   B. information   C. indictment   D. subpoena

Questions 10-15.

DIRECTIONS: Questions 10 through 15 are to be answered on the basis of the following fact pattern.

Jason's brother, Andrew, has been arrested. Jason appears at the courthouse as soon as he hears this news. He does not know why Andrew has been arrested, but suspects it may be related to his tumultuous relationship with his ex-girlfriend, who has filed a temporary restraining order against Andrew.

10. If Andrew was not arrested on a warrant, when will he be able to file a plea of guilty, not guilty, or no contest?
    A. At arraignment
    B. At trial
    C. At a preliminary conference
    D. At indictment

11. If Andrew is released from custody without a payment of money on the promise that he will appear for all hearings and for trial, the judge has released Andrew
    A. on his own recognizance
    B. with time served
    C. after a concurrent term
    D. on exculpatory evidence

12. In the alternative, if the judge sets bail for Andrew's release, he or she does so with the intent of
    A. punishing Andrew
    B. ensuring Andrew will appear for trial and all pre-trial hearings for which he must be present
    C. setting a fine dependent on the type of crime alleged
    D. releasing Andrew into the custody of his responsible brother, Jason

12._____

13. Which of the following should NOT be a factor a judge may use in deciding the amount of Andrew's bail?
    A. The risk of Andrew's fleeing
    B. The type of crime Andrew is alleged to have committed
    C. Andrew's age, race, and sex
    D. The safety of the community

13._____

14. During Andrew's initial appearance, the judge explains to Andrew that he has a right to a trial by jury.
    If Andrew does not want a trial by jury, what type of trial will he receive?
    A. An expedited trial   B. A bench trial
    C. A summation   D. An information

14._____

15. Andrew pleads no contest to the charges in his initial appearance.
    Andrew is effectively
    A. not admitting guilt or disputing the charge alleged
    B. admitting guilt
    C. denying the charge but admitting he will pay any fines incurred
    D. deferring his plea until a later date

15._____

Questions 16-19.

DIRECTIONS: Questions 16 through 19 are to be answered on the basis of the following fact pattern.

Jameson and Avery are neighbors. Jameson moved and purchased a home in the lot next to Avery's lot three months ago. Avery is suing Jameson for building a fence on Avery's property. Jameson attests the fence is actually being built on his own property and there is no boundary dispute. Jameson and Avery are both represented by counsel. A number of motions are filed by each party and discovery has been a lengthy process thus far.

16. Both parties serve each other requests to answer questions in writing under oath. Avery's attorney demands Jameson answer questions about the purchase of his home and dealings with the contractors building the fence. Jameson demands Avery answer questions about the property line dividing their property.
    This type of discovery is called
    A. interrogatories   B. demands
    C. summons   D. written decision

16._____

17. Avery's attorney would like to depose the property surveyor, Abe. Can Jameson and/or Jameson's attorney attend Abe's deposition?
    A. No, because Abe will be Avery's witness
    B. No, because Avery can share the information with Jameson's counsel at a later date
    C. No, because Abe's testimony may not be inadmissible in court so Jameson's presence would be futile
    D. Yes

17.____

18. Which of the following will NOT occur at the pre-trial conference between the parties?
    A. A deadline for discovery will be set.
    B. A trial date will be set.
    C. The judge will encourage stipulations between the parties.
    D. The judge will ask for oral arguments.

18.____

19. During discovery, both parties ascertain that Jameson built the fence on his side of the property line. Jameson's attorney asks the court to dismiss the case because there is no longer a legally sound basis to proceed. This request to the court is a motion to
    A. relinquish   B. dismiss   C. vacate   D. suppress

19.____

20. Which type of evidence suggests a fact by implication or inference?
    A. Exculpatory   B. Demandable
    C. Circumstantial   D. Ascertainable

20.____

21. Sam sued David civilly last September. Sam prevailed in the original suit. David has appealed. David is now the _____ and Sam is the _____.
    A. petitionery; respondent   B. appellant; appellee
    C. appellant; petitioner   D. respondent; appellee

21.____

22. If an appellate court remands a case back to the lower trial court, which of the following instructions may be imposed on the trial court.
    A. A new trial be held
    B. The trial court's judgment be modified or corrected
    C. The trial court reconsider the facts and/or the evidence presented
    D. All of the above

22.____

23. Which of the following motions may only be filed after all of the evidence has been presented?
    A. Motion in limine   B. Motion for directed verdict
    C. Motion for summary judgment D. Motion for admission

23.____

24. When is it permissible for parties to settle a suit?
    A. Before the trial begins   B. During the trial
    c. While the jury is deliberating D. All of the above

24.____

25. Summations are typically a part of _____ and discuss the evidence and the inferences that can be drawn from that evidence.
    A. closing arguments
    B. indictments
    C. hearings on the merits
    D. ex-parte communications

25.____

KEY (CORRECT ANSWERS)

1. C
2. A
3. B
4. A
5. D

6. B
7. B
8. D
9. D
10. A

11. A
12. B
13. C
14. B
15. A

16. A
17. D
18. D
19. B
20. C

21. B
22. D
23. B
24. D
25. A

TEST 3

DIRECTIONS: Each question or incomplete statement is followed by several suggested answers or completions. Select the one that BEST answers the question or completes the statement. *PRINT THE LETTER OF THE CORRECT ANSWER IN THE SPACE AT THE RIGHT.*

Questions 1-4.

DIRECTIONS: Questions 1 through 4 are to be answered on the basis of the following fact pattern.

Steven is on trial for embezzlement. The case is complex; there are eight witnesses for the prosecution and twelve witnesses for the defense, including character witnesses. Steven has filed a cross-claim against his former employer, and plaintiff, ABC Corp., Inc. for defamation of character. Steven maintains that he never stole a dime from ABC Corp., Inc. and wants ABC Corp., Inc. to issue him a public apology when the trial is over.

1. The BEST place to refer back to the testimony of one witness is 1.____
   A. the docket
   B. the judge's notes
   C. the stenographer's transcript
   D. clerk notes

2. Steven's attorney presents evidence that his client was not working on the days the theft from ABC Corp. allegedly occurred. 2.____
   What kind of evidence is Steven's counsel presenting to the court?
   A. Alibi
   B. Exculpatory
   C. Exclusionary
   D. Exemplary

3. Alexandra, a friend of Steven, testifies for the prosecution in Steven's case. Alexandra testifies that Steven told her that he embezzled money from ABC Corp. Steven's attorney objects to Alexandra's testimony because it is 3.____
   A. exculpatory   B. hearsay   C. untrue   D. impeachment

4. At the close of Steven's trial, oral arguments are made by _____ to the court, summarizing their position on the evidence that has been presented and their theories on the case in its entirety. 4.____
   A. jurors   B. plaintiffs   C. attorneys   D. defense

Questions 5-8.

DIRECTIONS: Questions 5 through 8 are to be answered on the basis of the following fact pattern.

April 16 is turning out to be a very busy day at the courthouse. In the morning, three cases were withdrawn by the plaintiff without a hearing, six cases were dismissed without prejudice by the judge, and two cases were settled out of court.

5. How many were decided by the judge on April 16? 5.____
   A. 0   B. 2   C. 6   D. 3

6. How many cases were heard before the judge?　　　　　　　　　　　　　　　　　　6.____
   A. 3　　　　　　B. 6　　　　　　C. 2　　　　　　D. 8

7. How many cases would the court reporter need to be present for?　　　　　　　7.____
   A. 6　　　　　　B. 3　　　　　　C. 2　　　　　　D. 8

8. How many of the cases were awarded damages?　　　　　　　　　　　　　　　　8.____
   A. 2　　　　　　B. 6　　　　　　C. 3　　　　　　D. 0

Questions 9-12.

DIRECTIONS: Questions 9 through 12 are to be answered on the basis of the following fact pattern.

Miranda has initiated a lawsuit against her former friend, Anne, for breach of contract. Miranda referred Anne's interior design services to Miranda's boss. Anne went to Miranda's boss' house for an initial consultation and, even though Anne agreed to design three rooms in the house, she never followed through with the contract. Miranda is incredibly embarrassed by the entire situation. Anne, however, maintains that she has a reasonable excuse for not finishing the work.

9. In addition to money damages, Miranda would also like the court to compel　　9.____
   Anne to execute the contract or, in other words, actually design the rooms.
   This remedy is deemed
   A. compulsion under order　　　　　B. specific performance
   C. remedy at law　　　　　　　　　　D. joint and several liability

10. Miranda alleges that she suffered pain and suffering from Anne's inability to　　10.____
    execute the contract.
    What type of damages are pain and suffering categorized as?
    A. Punitive　　　　B. Special　　　　C. Specific　　　　D. Compensatory

11. Miranda lives in New York. Anne lives in New Jersey. Miranda's boss　　　　11.____
    lives in Connecticut. When Miranda files suit in New York, the judge initially
    indicates that she does not have
    A. authority　　　　B. jurisdiction　　　　C. venue　　　　D. domicile

12. The contract that is alleged to have been breached exists between Anne and　　12.____
    Miranda's boss, not Miranda. Therefore, there is no legal cause of action for
    the case to proceed. Miranda's boss is free to file the claim against Anne at a
    later date if she so chooses.
    The court will
    A. dismiss the action without prejudice
    B. deny the action without prejudice
    C. sustain the action
    D. abdicate as necessary

13. Nominal damages are
    A. damages awarded in name only, indicating no substantial harm was done
    B. damages to recompense the injured for the infliction of emotional distress
    C. damages to recompense the initiator of the lawsuit
    D. a reimbursement of filing fees, awarded to the person who can prove they are injured

14. The type of recovery being sought by the plaintiff is known as the
    A. order   B. punishment   C. remedy   D. issue

15. Robert approaches the clerk's desk in a panic. He says that he filed a lawsuit against his cousin, Mike, but neglected to add his cousin's friend, Roy, to the suit.
    What action is Robert attempting to take?
    A. Amending the complaint
    B. Adding an addendum to the summons
    C. Re-issuing a summons
    D. Redacting the answer

Questions 16-20.

DIRECTIONS: Questions 16 through 20 are to be answered on the basis of the following fact pattern.

Daniel and Patrick sue one another civilly. Daniel sues Patrick for intentional infliction of emotional distress and Patrick countersues Daniel for assault. Both causes of action stem from a physical altercation which took place at a youth hockey game where Daniel's and Patrick's sons played against one another. At trial, the judge found that Daniel started the fight and attacked Patrick and found, by extension, that Patrick was not a contributor in the altercation.

Daniel appealed the decision to an appellate court. Daniel's attorney argued that the trial court erred, as a matter of law, in finding that Daniel was the sole initiator of the altercation and ignored evidence to the contrary. Appellate courts generally render decisions by a panel. The panel in Daniel's appeal was comprised of three justices. The appellate court agreed with the trial court's finding of fault.

16. The ultimate disposition of this case was the appellate court
    A. affirmed the lower court's decision
    B. remanded the lower court's decision
    C. reversed the lower court's decision
    D. acquitted Daniel of all charges

17. An opinion from the entire panel of justices is known as a
    A. per curiam decision   B. affirmative decision
    C. stare decisis   D. en banc order

18. One of the judges agrees with the decision of the court, but disagrees with the reasoning of the conclusion. This judge decides to write his own opinion. This is deemed a
    A. dissenting opinion
    B. remedial decision
    C. concurring opinion
    D. recurrent opinion

19. Suppose that one of the judges disagrees entirely with the ruling. How will the judgment be altered because of the disagreement? The judgment
    A. is unaffected because the majority voted in agreement with the trial court
    B. is unaffected because this judge did not author a dissenting opinion
    C. is unaffected because oral arguments were not made before the panel
    D. will be overturned

20. The appellate court still requires _____, even if it is established by the trial court, known as original _____.
    A. domicile; venue
    B. venue; jurisdiction
    C. jurisdiction; jurisdiction
    D. jurisdiction; domicile

21. The legal theory upon which a case is based is called a
    A. basis
    B. decisis
    C. cause of action
    D. precedent

Questions 22-25.

DIRECTIONS: Questions 22 through 25 are to be answered on the basis of the following fact pattern.

Last July, Sarah stole Alexis's car and took it for a joyride along Main Street. After a long joyride, Sarah decided to pick up Ashley at Ashley's apartment. Although Ashley asked when Sarah bought a new car, Sarah lied and told Ashley that it was her aunt's car that she borrowed with permission. Sarah and Ashley went on another joyride, this time driving up to 90 miles per hour on the highways around town. After three hours, Ashley asked to go home and Sarah obliged. After Sarah dropped Ashley back off at her apartment, Sarah sped through a busy intersection and crashed the car. The car was totaled.
Alexis has filed a lawsuit against both Sarah and Ashley.

22. Alexis is determined to sue both Sarah and Ashley for conversion, or the wrongful act of dominion or control over another person's property. However, after meeting with her attorney, Alexis decided she may not be able to prove each _____ of the alleged crime against Ashley.
    A. stage   B. element   C. circumstance   D. remedy

23. After Alexis initiated her lawsuit against Sarah and Ashley, Ashley requested the court remove her from the lawsuit altogether. She attested that she could not have participated in a crime if she did not know the car was stolen. Her request to the court will come in the form of a(n)
    A. notice   B. motion   C. termination   D. demand

24. Ashley's attorney asks the judge to instruct the jury that it can consider mitigating factors in rendering a verdict against Ashley.
An example of a mitigating factor in this scenario would MOST likely be
   A. Ashley does not known Alexis
   B. Sarah is no longer friends with Alexis
   C. Ashley asked Sarah about the origins of the car and Sarah's reply was untruthful
   D. Ashley and Sarah were working in cahoots to steal Alexis's car

25. During the time of the crime Sarah was a minor. A minor is legally defined as
   A. someone who cannot think for themselves
   B. anyone under 21
   C. a legally emancipated individual
   D. an infant or individual under the age of legal competence

KEY (CORRECT ANSWERS)

1.	C		11.	B
2.	B		12.	A
3.	B		13.	A
4.	C		14.	C
5.	C		15.	A
6.	B		16.	A
7.	A		17.	A
8.	D		18.	C
9.	B		19.	A
10.	D		20.	C

21. C
22. B
23. B
24. C
25. D

TEST 4

DIRECTIONS: Each question or incomplete statement is followed by several suggested answers or completions. Select the one that BEST answers the question or completes the statement. *PRINT THE LETTER OF THE CORRECT ANSWER IN THE SPACE AT THE RIGHT.*

Questions 1-4.

DIRECTIONS: Questions 1 through 4 are to be answered on the basis of the following fact pattern.

A complex civil litigation suit is set to begin between ABC Insurance Corp. and DEF Indemnity Corp. Adam represents ABC Insurance and Jane represents DEF Indemnity Corp. Multiple extensions have been granted to either side to conduct more extensive discovery. At the last conference scheduled before trial, the presiding judge is notably frustrated at the requested delays from both Adam and Jane. The presiding judge would like both parties to stipulate to as many points as possible.

1. Adam and Jane appear in the permanent record as _____ unless either are withdrawn or are otherwise removed from the case.
   A. attorneys in time
   B. attorneys of record
   C. attorneys of the case
   D. permanent attorneys

2. The judge asks whether the parties have attempted to settle this matter in another forum, such as binding _____.
   A. decision-making
   B. arbitration
   C. neutral court
   D. judgment arena

3. While the judge would like the parties to settle, he quickly realizes that it is not a possibility between these two parties. Adam and Jane continue to argue about various issues including expert witnesses. Adam argues that Jane's expert witness, who will testify about financial crimes, is a quack. In response, Jane offers that her witness be _____, or testify under oath at a date prior to trial.
   A. sworn in   B. indemnified   C. deposed   D. saddled

4. Which of the following is the LEAST appropriate behavior of the judge during a pre-trial conference?
   A. Providing advice on Adam or Jane's legal strategy for trial
   B. Asking the parties to stipulate to the facts
   C. Remaining indifferent about the witnesses each party plans to call at trial
   D. Setting a date for trial more than three months away

5. A lawsuit with a single cause of action being breach of contract will be classified as what type of suit?
   A. Criminal   B. Divisional   C. Situational   D. Civil

6. Sheila's mother passed away last week. She comes to the courthouse and asks about the probate process. You inform her that probate may not be necessary if she is the person named in the will as the individual who will administer her mother's estate. This individual is otherwise known as the
   A. administrator   B. guarantor   C. creditor   D. executor

7. Brandy would like her juvenile record expunged. What is she seeking to do? She is requesting
   A. her record, or a portion of her record, be removed
   B. her record be sealed
   C. her record be unsealed
   D. to make her record unavailable to creditors

8. Having never met Jamie, a pro se litigant, Judge Smith strikes up a friendly conversation about the recent political climate in the elevator with him on the way to the courtroom. In the courtroom that afternoon, Jamie enters his appearance and says, "You and I are clearly already on the same page, Judge" in open court. Jamie's adversary, Courtney, requests that the judge recuses himself from the case. Why?
   A. Jamie and Judge Smith's political affiliations are unsavory.
   B. Judge Smith is clearly biased as evidenced by Jamie's comment.
   C. Judge Smith and Jamie have partaken in en banc communications.
   D. Judicial discrimination is appropriate if a conflict of interest would affect a judge's ruling.

9. Emily appears at court with a crumbled notice in her hands. She has a complaint in her hands and indicates that she never answered or responded to the complaint, hoping it would go away or resolve itself.
   Emily is currently
   A. in default   B. owes restitution
   C. in declaratory judgment   D. subsidiary

10. A conditional release from incarceration is known as
    A. an expungement   B. a restitution
    C. parole   D. reduced sentence

11. Tom paid a contractor to cut down a large pine tree in front of his house. The tree had grown so tall that it has started to interfere with the power lines running parallel to the street. As the contractor cut down the tree, a large gust of wind blew and the tree crashed down on top of his neighbor, Dane's, roof. Dane is suing Tom for failure to exercise the degree of care that a reasonable person would have exercised in the same circumstance.
    Dane is suing Tom for
    A. lack of judgment   B. breach of contract
    C. negligence   D. conversion

12. Lawyers are generally prohibited from asking _____ questions of their own witnesses because they are suggestive, or prompt, the witness to answer in a certain way.
    A. leading   B. direct   C. cross   D. sustainable

13. One process that is generally private, and not heard in open court, is(are)
    A. testimony of expert witnesses
    B. swearing in of jurors
    C. objections
    D. plea bargaining

14. The burden of proof in a civil case is _____ stringent than that in a criminal case.
    A. less   B. more   C. equally   D. substantially

15. May jurors consider arguments made during an attorney's opening or closing arguments as evidence or fact?
    A. Yes, but only if compelling
    B. Yes, but only under the circumstances explained by the judge
    C. Yes, unconditionally
    D. No

16. In reviewing the court transcript, which of the following is the attorney LEAST likely to find?
    A. The judge's opinions on the case
    B. Testimony of the petitioner
    C. Attorneys of record
    D. Names of the expert witnesses

17. A mandatory injunction has the effect of
    A. requiring a party to do a particular act
    B. providing the option of a party to do a particular act
    C. requiring a party to report their actions
    D. providing the party an option to report their actions

18. James approaches the clerk's desk and asks how, generally, judges make their decisions on legal matters.
    The MOST correct answer would be: Based on
    A. case law, or the body of all court decisions which govern or provide precedent on the same legal issue before the judge
    B. case law, personal opinion, and oral arguments by attorneys
    C. case law, oral arguments by attorneys, and the defendant's rap sheet
    D. "stare decisis" or that which has already been decided

19. Which of the following individuals is LEAST likely to serve on a jury?
    A. Susan, who has been called numerous times but never served on a jury
    B. Bill, a supporter of labor unions and freelance political columnist
    C. Gary, who served on a murder trial 10 years ago
    D. Amy, a 16-year-old genius who just finished her junior year of college

20. If a grand jury decides there is enough evidence to move forward with criminal charges against a group or individual, they return a(n)
    A. information   B. indictment   C. warrant   D. seizure

21. When an attorney attempts to reduce the credibility of the other side's witness, they are said to be trying to _____ the witness.
    A. objectify   B. anger   C. impeach   D. frustrate

22. During a lengthy murder trial, it is discovered that two of the jurors have been romantically involved. They have conspired with one another to enter votes of "not guilty" and attempt to sway other jurors in their favor in an attempt to close out deliberations early.
    What is the likely outcome of the trial?
    A. Hung jury   B. Mistrial
    C. Acquittal   D. Defensive charge

23. The judge's charge to the jury is also known as
    A. voir dire   B. en banc
    C. jury instructions   D. sua sponte

24. Who is MOST likely to deliver the sentence to the convicted?
    A. Bailiff   B. Jury
    C. Judge   D. Jury foreperson

25. A motion for directed verdict is made
    A. without the jury present
    B. with only the jury foreperson present
    C. with the entire jury present
    D. with only the alternate jurors present

KEY (CORRECT ANSWERS)

1.	B	11.	C
2.	B	12.	A
3.	C	13.	D
4.	A	14.	A
5.	D	15.	D
6.	D	16.	A
7.	A	17.	A
8.	D	18.	A
9.	A	19.	D
10.	C	20.	B

21. C
22. B
23. C
24. C
25. A

COURTROOM TERMS

A/K/A: Acronym that stands for "also known as" and introduces any alternative or assumed names or aliases of an individual. A term to indicate another name by which a person is known.

Arraignment: The bringing of a defendant before the court to answer the matters charged against him in an indictment or information. The defendant is read the charges and must respond with his plea.

Arrest: Deprivation of one's liberty by legal authority.

Bail: An amount of money set by the court to procure the release of a person from legal custody; this money is to be forfeited if the defendant fails to appear for trial.

Beyond a Reasonable Doubt: The standard of proof required for a finding of guilty in a criminal matter. Satisfied to a moral certainty. This is a higher standard of proof than that required in a civil matter (preponderance of the evidence).

Co-Defendant: Any additional defendant or respondent in the same case.

Confession: A voluntary statement made by a person charged with a crime wherein said person acknowledges his/her guilt of the offense charged and discloses participation in the act.

Controlled Dangerous Substance: That group of legally designated drugs, which, by statute, it is illegal to possess or distribute.

Criminal complaint: The initial written notice to a defendant that he/she is being charged with a public offense.

Due Process of Law: The exercise of the powers of the government with the safeguards for the protection of individual rights as set forth in the constitution, statutes, and common case law.

Felony: A crime of a more serious nature than a misdemeanor, the exact nature of which is defined by state statute and which is punishable by a term of imprisonment exceeding one year or by death.

Grand Jury: A jury of inquiry whose duty is to receive complaints and accusations in criminal cases, hear the evidence presented on the part of the state, and determine whether to indict (see "indictment" below).

Impeach: As used in the Law of Evidence, to call into question the truthfulness of a witness, by means of introducing evidence to discredit him or her.

Indictment: A written accusation presented by a grand jury after having been presented with evidence, charging that a person named therein has done some act, or has been guilty of some omission that by law is a public offense.

Miranda Warnings: The compulsory advisement of a person's rights prior to any custodial interrogation; these include: a) the right to remain silent; b) that any statement made may be used against him/her; c) the right to an attorney; d) the appointment of counsel if the accused cannot afford his or her own attorney. Unless these rights are given, any evidence obtained in an interrogation cannot be used in the individual's trial against him/her.

Misdemeanor: Offense lower than felony and generally punishable by a fine or imprisonment other than in a penitentiary.

Motion to Quash: Application to the court to set aside the complaint, indictment or subpoena due to a lack of probable cause to arrest the defendant, or in matters heard by a grand jury, due to evidence not properly presented to the grand jury.

Motion to Sever: Application to the court made when there are two defendants charged with the same crimes or who acted jointly in the commission of a crime, when their attorneys feel it would be in their best interest if they had separate trials.

Motion to Suppress Evidence: Application to the court to prevent evidence from being presented at trial when said evidence has been obtained by illegal means. It applies to physical evidence, statements made by defendant when not advised by counsel or through wiretapping, prior convictions, etc..

Parole: A conditional release from custody at the discretion of the paroling authority prior to his or her completing the prison sentence imposed. During said release the offender is required to observe conditions of this status under the supervision of a parole agency.

Plea: A defendant's formal answer in court to the charges contained in a charging document.

Guilty: A plea by the defendant in which he acknowledges guilt either of the offense charged or of a less serious offense pursuant to an agreement with the prosecuting attorney. It should be understood, however, that the court may not be obliged to recognize this.

Nolo Contendere: A plea that is admissible in some jurisdictions, in which the defendant states that he does not contest the charges against him. Also called "no contest", this plea has the same effect as a guilty plea, except that it cannot be used against the defendant in civil actions arising out of the same incident which gave rise to the criminal charges.

Not Guilty: A plea of innocence by the defendant.

Not Guilty by Reason of Insanity: A plea that is sometimes entered in conjunction with the "not guilty" plea.

Double Jeopardy: A plea entered by a defendant who has been tried for an offense wherein he asserts that he cannot be tried a second time for said offense, unless he successfully secured a new trial after an appeal, or after a motion for a new trial was granted by the trial court.

Police Report: The official report made by any police officer involved with the incident or appearing after the incident, setting forth the officer's observations and statements of parties and witnesses. It can be used as evidence in a trial.

Pre-Trial Intervention: Utilized in some states when a defendant is accused of a first offense, to divert the defendant from the criminal justice system.

Probation: To allow a person convicted of a minor offense to go at large, under a suspension of sentence, during good behavior, and generally under the supervision of a probation officer.

Prosecutor: The attorney who prosecutes defendants for crimes, in the name of the government.

Search Warrant: A written order, issued by the court, directing the police to search a specified location for particular personal property (stolen or illegally possessed).

Speedy Trial: Mandate by the government that all criminal trials must take place within a specified time after arrest.

Writ of Habeas Corpus: A mandate issued from a court requiring that an individual be brought before the court.

GLOSSARY OF LEGAL TERMS

TABLE OF CONTENTS

	Page
Action ... Affiant	1
Affidavit ... At Bar	2
At Issue ... Burden of Proof	3
Business ... Commute	4
Complainant ... Conviction	5
Cooperative ... Demur (v.)	6
Demurrage ... Endorsement	7
Enjoin ... Facsimile	8
Factor ... Guilty	9
Habeas Corpus ... Incumbrance	10
Indemnify ... Laches	11
Landlord and Tenant ... Malice	12
Mandamus ... Obiter Dictum	13
Object (v.) ... Perjury	14
Perpetuity ... Proclamation	15
Proffered Evidence ... Referee	16
Referendum ... Stare Decisis	17
State ... Term	18
Testamentary ... Warrant (Warranty) (v.)	19
Warrant (n.) ... Zoning	20

GLOSSARY OF LEGAL TERMS
A

ACTION - "Action" includes a civil action and a criminal action.
A FORTIORI - A term meaning you can reason one thing from the existence of certain facts.
A POSTERIORI - From what goes after; from effect to cause.
A PRIORI - From what goes before; from cause to effect.
AB INITIO - From the beginning.
ABATE - To diminish or put an end to.
ABET - To encourage the commission of a crime.
ABEYANCE - Suspension, temporary suppression.
ABIDE - To accept the consequences of.
ABJURE - To renounce; give up.
ABRIDGE - To reduce; contract; diminish.
ABROGATE - To annul, repeal, or destroy.
ABSCOND - To hide or absent oneself to avoid legal action.
ABSTRACT - A summary.
ABUT - To border on, to touch.
ACCESS - Approach; in real property law it means the right of the owner of property to the use of the highway or road next to his land, without obstruction by intervening property owners.
ACCESSORY - In criminal law, it means the person who contributes or aids in the commission of a crime.
ACCOMMODATED PARTY - One to whom credit is extended on the strength of another person signing a commercial paper.
ACCOMMODATION PAPER - A commercial paper to which the accommodating party has put his name.
ACCOMPLICE - In criminal law, it means a person who together with the principal offender commits a crime.
ACCORD - An agreement to accept something different or less than that to which one is entitled, which extinguishes the entire obligation.
ACCOUNT - A statement of mutual demands in the nature of debt and credit between parties.
ACCRETION - The act of adding to a thing; in real property law, it means gradual accumulation of land by natural causes.
ACCRUE - To grow to; to be added to.
ACKNOWLEDGMENT - The act of going before an official authorized to take acknowledgments, and acknowledging an act as one's own.
ACQUIESCENCE - A silent appearance of consent.
ACQUIT - To legally determine the innocence of one charged with a crime.
AD INFINITUM - Indefinitely.
AD LITEM - For the suit.
AD VALOREM - According to value.
ADJECTIVE LAW - Rules of procedure.
ADJUDICATION - The judgment given in a case.
ADMIRALTY - Court having jurisdiction over maritime cases.
ADULT - Sixteen years old or over (in criminal law).
ADVANCE - In commercial law, it means to pay money or render other value before it is due.
ADVERSE - Opposed; contrary.
ADVOCATE - (v.) To speak in favor of;
          (n.) One who assists, defends, or pleads for another.
AFFIANT - A person who makes and signs an affidavit.

AFFIDAVIT - A written and sworn to declaration of facts, voluntarily made.
AFFINITY- The relationship between persons through marriage with the kindred of each other; distinguished from consanguinity, which is the relationship by blood.
AFFIRM - To ratify; also when an appellate court affirms a judgment, decree, or order, it means that it is valid and right and must stand as rendered in the lower court.
AFOREMENTIONED; AFORESAID - Before or already said.
AGENT - One who represents and acts for another.
AID AND COMFORT - To help; encourage.
ALIAS - A name not one's true name.
ALIBI - A claim of not being present at a certain place at a certain time.
ALLEGE - To assert.
ALLOTMENT - A share or portion.
AMBIGUITY - Uncertainty; capable of being understood in more than one way.
AMENDMENT - Any language made or proposed as a change in some principal writing.
AMICUS CURIAE - A friend of the court; one who has an interest in a case, although not a party in the case, who volunteers advice upon matters of law to the judge. For example, a brief amicus curiae.
AMORTIZATION - To provide for a gradual extinction of (a future obligation) in advance of maturity, especially, by periodical contributions to a sinking fund which will be adequate to discharge a debt or make a replacement when it becomes necessary.
ANCILLARY - Aiding, auxiliary.
ANNOTATION - A note added by way of comment or explanation.
ANSWER - A written statement made by a defendant setting forth the grounds of his defense.
ANTE - Before.
ANTE MORTEM - Before death.
APPEAL - The removal of a case from a lower court to one of superior jurisdiction for the purpose of obtaining a review.
APPEARANCE - Coming into court as a party to a suit.
APPELLANT - The party who takes an appeal from one court or jurisdiction to another (appellate) court for review.
APPELLEE - The party against whom an appeal is taken.
APPROPRIATE - To make a thing one's own.
APPROPRIATION - Prescribing the destination of a thing; the act of the legislature designating a particular fund, to be applied to some object of government expenditure.
APPURTENANT - Belonging to; accessory or incident to.
ARBITER - One who decides a dispute; a referee.
ARBITRARY - Unreasoned; not governed by any fixed rules or standard.
ARGUENDO - By way of argument.
ARRAIGN - To call the prisoner before the court to answer to a charge.
ASSENT - A declaration of willingness to do something in compliance with a request.
ASSERT - Declare.
ASSESS - To fix the rate or amount.
ASSIGN - To transfer; to appoint; to select for a particular purpose.
ASSIGNEE - One who receives an assignment.
ASSIGNOR - One who makes an assignment.
AT BAR - Before the court.

AT ISSUE - When parties in an action come to a point where one asserts something and the other denies it.
ATTACH - Seize property by court order and sometimes arrest a person.
ATTEST - To witness a will, etc.; act of attestation.
AVERMENT - A positive statement of facts.

B

BAIL - To obtain the release of a person from legal custody by giving security and promising that he shall appear in court; to deliver (goods, etc.) in trust to a person for a special purpose.
BAILEE - One to whom personal property is delivered under a contract of bailment.
BAILMENT - Delivery of personal property to another to be held for a certain purpose and to be returned when the purpose is accomplished.
BAILOR - The party who delivers goods to another, under a contract of bailment.
BANC (OR BANK) - Bench; the place where a court sits permanently or regularly; also the assembly of all the judges of a court.
BANKRUPT - An insolvent person, technically, one declared to be bankrupt after a bankruptcy proceeding.
BAR - The legal profession.
BARRATRY - Exciting groundless judicial proceedings.
BARTER - A contract by which parties exchange goods for other goods.
BATTERY - Illegal interfering with another's person.
BEARER - In commercial law, it means the person in possession of a commercial paper which is payable to the bearer.
BENCH - The court itself or the judge.
BENEFICIARY - A person benefiting under a will, trust, or agreement.
BEST EVIDENCE RULE, THE - Except as otherwise provided by statute, no evidence other than the writing itself is admissible to prove the content of a writing. This section shall be known and may be cited as the best evidence rule.
BEQUEST - A gift of personal property under a will.
BILL - A formal written statement of complaint to a court of justice; also, a draft of an act of the legislature before it becomes a law; also, accounts for goods sold, services rendered, or work done.
BONA FIDE - In or with good faith; honestly.
BOND - An instrument by which the maker promises to pay a sum of money to another, usually providing that upon performances of a certain condition the obligation shall be void.
BOYCOTT - A plan to prevent the carrying on of a business by wrongful means.
BREACH - The breaking or violating of a law, or the failure to carry out a duty.
BRIEF - A written document, prepared by a lawyer to serve as the basis of an argument upon a case in court, usually an appellate court.
BURDEN OF PRODUCING EVIDENCE - The obligation of a party to introduce evidence sufficient to avoid a ruling against him on the issue.
BURDEN OF PROOF - The obligation of a party to establish by evidence a requisite degree of belief concerning a fact in the mind of the trier of fact or the court. The burden of proof may require a party to raise a reasonable doubt concerning the existence of nonexistence of a fact or that he establish the existence or nonexistence of a fact by a preponderance of the evidence, by clear and convincing proof, or by proof beyond a reasonable doubt.

Except as otherwise provided by law, the burden of proof requires proof by a preponderance of the evidence.

BUSINESS, A - Shall include every kind of business, profession, occupation, calling or operation of institutions, whether carried on for profit or not.

BY-LAWS - Regulations, ordinances, or rules enacted by a corporation, association, etc., for its own government.

C

CANON - A doctrine; also, a law or rule, of a church or association in particular.

CAPIAS - An order to arrest.

CAPTION - In a pleading, deposition or other paper connected with a case in court, it is the heading or introductory clause which shows the names of the parties, name of the court, number of the case on the docket or calendar, etc.

CARRIER - A person or corporation undertaking to transport persons or property.

CASE - A general term for an action, cause, suit, or controversy before a judicial body.

CAUSE - A suit, litigation or action before a court.

CAVEAT EMPTOR - Let the buyer beware. This term expresses the rule that the purchaser of an article must examine, judge, and test it for himself, being bound to discover any obvious defects or imperfections.

CERTIFICATE - A written representation that some legal formality has been complied with.

CERTIORARI - To be informed of; the name of a writ issued by a superior court directing the lower court to send up to the former the record and proceedings of a case.

CHANGE OF VENUE - To remove place of trial from one place to another.

CHARGE - An obligation or duty; a formal complaint; an instruction of the court to the jury upon a case.

CHARTER - (n.) The authority by virtue of which an organized body acts;
    (v.) in mercantile law, it means to hire or lease a vehicle or vessel for transportation.

CHATTEL - An article of personal property.

CHATTEL MORTGAGE - A mortgage on personal property.

CIRCUIT - A division of the country, for the administration of justice; a geographical area served by a court.

CITATION - The act of the court by which a person is summoned or cited; also, a reference to legal authority.

CIVIL (ACTIONS)- It indicates the private rights and remedies of individuals in contrast to the word "criminal" (actions) which relates to prosecution for violation of laws.

CLAIM (n.) - Any demand held or asserted as of right.

CODICIL - An addition to a will.

CODIFY - To arrange the laws of a country into a code.

COGNIZANCE - Notice or knowledge.

COLLATERAL - By the side; accompanying; an article or thing given to secure performance of a promise.

COMITY - Courtesy; the practice by which one court follows the decision of another court on the same question.

COMMIT - To perform, as an act; to perpetrate, as a crime; to send a person to prison.

COMMON LAW - As distinguished from law created by the enactment of the legislature (called statutory law), it relates to those principles and rules of action which derive their authority solely from usages and customs of immemorial antiquity, particularly with reference to the ancient unwritten law of England. The written pronouncements of the common law are found in court decisions.

COMMUTE - Change punishment to one less severe.

COMPLAINANT - One who applies to the court for legal redress.
COMPLAINT - The pleading of a plaintiff in a civil action; or a charge that a person has committed a specified offense.
COMPROMISE - An arrangement for settling a dispute by agreement.
CONCUR - To agree, consent.
CONCURRENT - Running together, at the same time.
CONDEMNATION - Taking private property for public use on payment therefor.
CONDITION - Mode or state of being; a qualification or restriction.
CONDUCT - Active and passive behavior; both verbal and nonverbal.
CONFESSION - Voluntary statement of guilt of crime.
CONFIDENTIAL COMMUNICATION BETWEEN CLIENT AND LAWYER - Information transmitted between a client and his lawyer in the course of that relationship and in confidence by a means which, so far as the client is aware, discloses the information to no third persons other than those who are present to further the interest of the client in the consultation or those to whom disclosure is reasonably necessary for the transmission of the information or the accomplishment of the purpose for which the lawyer is consulted, and includes a legal opinion formed and the advice given by the lawyer in the course of that relationship.
CONFRONTATION - Witness testifying in presence of defendant.
CONSANGUINITY - Blood relationship.
CONSIGN - To give in charge; commit; entrust; to send or transmit goods to a merchant, factor, or agent for sale.
CONSIGNEE - One to whom a consignment is made.
CONSIGNOR - One who sends or makes a consignment.
CONSPIRACY - In criminal law, it means an agreement between two or more persons to commit an unlawful act.
CONSPIRATORS - Persons involved in a conspiracy.
CONSTITUTION - The fundamental law of a nation or state.
CONSTRUCTION OF GENDERS - The masculine gender includes the feminine and neuter.
CONSTRUCTION OF SINGULAR AND PLURAL - The singular number includes the plural; and the plural, the singular.
CONSTRUCTION OF TENSES - The present tense includes the past and future tenses; and the future, the present.
CONSTRUCTIVE - An act or condition assumed from other parts or conditions.
CONSTRUE - To ascertain the meaning of language.
CONSUMMATE - To complete.
CONTIGUOUS - Adjoining; touching; bounded by.
CONTINGENT - Possible, but not assured; dependent upon some condition.
CONTINUANCE - The adjournment or postponement of an action pending in a court.
CONTRA - Against, opposed to; contrary.
CONTRACT - An agreement between two or more persons to do or not to do a particular thing.
CONTROVERT - To dispute, deny.
CONVERSION - Dealing with the personal property of another as if it were one's own, without right.
CONVEYANCE - An instrument transferring title to land.
CONVICTION - Generally, the result of a criminal trial which ends in a judgment or sentence that the defendant is guilty as charged.

COOPERATIVE - A cooperative is a voluntary organization of persons with a common interest, formed and operated along democratic lines for the purpose of supplying services at cost to its members and other patrons, who contribute both capital and business.
CORPUS DELICTI - The body of a crime; the crime itself.
CORROBORATE - To strengthen; to add weight by additional evidence.
COUNTERCLAIM - A claim presented by a defendant in opposition to or deduction from the claim of the plaintiff.
COUNTY - Political subdivision of a state.
COVENANT - Agreement.
CREDIBLE - Worthy of belief.
CREDITOR - A person to whom a debt is owing by another person, called the "debtor."
CRIMINAL ACTION - Includes criminal proceedings.
CRIMINAL INFORMATION - Same as complaint.
CRITERION (sing.)
CRITERIA (plural) - A means or tests for judging; a standard or standards.
CROSS-EXAMINATION - Examination of a witness by a party other than the direct examiner upon a matter that is within the scope of the direct examination of the witness.
CULPABLE - Blamable.
CY-PRES - As near as (possible). The rule of *cy-pres* is a rule for the construction of instruments in equity by which the intention of the party is carried out *as near as may be*, when it would be impossible or illegal to give it literal effect.

D

DAMAGES - A monetary compensation, which may be recovered in the courts by any person who has suffered loss, or injury, whether to his person, property or rights through the unlawful act or omission or negligence of another.
DECLARANT - A person who makes a statement.
DE FACTO - In fact; actually but without legal authority.
DE JURE - Of right; legitimate; lawful.
DE MINIMIS - Very small or trifling.
DE NOVO - Anew; afresh; a second time.
DEBT - A specified sum of money owing to one person from another, including not only the obligation of the debtor to pay, but the right of the creditor to receive and enforce payment.
DECEDENT - A dead person.
DECISION - A judgment or decree pronounced by a court in determination of a case.
DECREE - An order of the court, determining the rights of all parties to a suit.
DEED - A writing containing a contract sealed and delivered; particularly to convey real property.
DEFALCATION - Misappropriation of funds.
DEFAMATION - Injuring one's reputation by false statements.
DEFAULT - The failure to fulfill a duty, observe a promise, discharge an obligation, or perform an agreement.
DEFENDANT - The person defending or denying; the party against whom relief or recovery is sought in an action or suit.
DEFRAUD - To practice fraud; to cheat or trick.
DELEGATE (v.)- To entrust to the care or management of another.
DELICTUS - A crime.
DEMUR (v.) - To dispute the sufficiency in law of the pleading of the other side.

DEMURRAGE - In maritime law, it means, the sum fixed or allowed as remuneration to the owners of a ship for the detention of their vessel beyond the number of days allowed for loading and unloading or for sailing; also used in railroad terminology.
DENIAL - A form of pleading; refusing to admit the truth of a statement, charge, etc.
DEPONENT - One who gives testimony under oath reduced to writing.
DEPOSITION - Testimony given under oath outside of court for use in court or for the purpose of obtaining information in preparation for trial of a case.
DETERIORATION - A degeneration such as from decay, corrosion or disintegration.
DETRIMENT - Any loss or harm to person or property.
DEVIATION - A turning aside.
DEVISE - A gift of real property by the last will and testament of the donor.
DICTUM (sing.)
DICTA (plural) - Any statements made by the court in an opinion concerning some rule of law not necessarily involved nor essential to the determination of the case.
DIRECT EVIDENCE - Evidence that directly proves a fact, without an inference or presumption, and which in itself if true, conclusively establishes that fact.
DIRECT EXAMINATION - The first examination of a witness upon a matter that is not within the scope of a previous examination of the witness.
DISAFFIRM - To repudiate.
DISMISS - In an action or suit, it means to dispose of the case without any further consideration or hearing.
DISSENT - To denote disagreement of one or more judges of a court with the decision passed by the majority upon a case before them.
DOCKET (n.) - A formal record, entered in brief, of the proceedings in a court.
DOCTRINE - A rule, principle, theory of law.
DOMICILE - That place where a man has his true, fixed and permanent home to which whenever he is absent he has the intention of returning.
DRAFT (n.) - A commercial paper ordering payment of money drawn by one person on another.
DRAWEE - The person who is requested to pay the money.
DRAWER - The person who draws the commercial paper and addresses it to the drawee.
DUPLICATE - A counterpart produced by the same impression as the original enlargements and miniatures, or by mechanical or electronic re-recording, or by chemical reproduction, or by other equivalent technique which accurately reproduces the original.
DURESS - Use of force to compel performance or non-performance of an act.

E

EASEMENT - A liberty, privilege, or advantage without profit, in the lands of another.
EGRESS - Act or right of going out or leaving; emergence.
EIUSDEM GENERIS - Of the same kind, class or nature. A rule used in the construction of language in a legal document.
EMBEZZLEMENT - To steal; to appropriate fraudulently to one's own use property entrusted to one's care.
EMBRACERY - Unlawful attempt to influence jurors, etc., but not by offering value.
EMINENT DOMAIN - The right of a state to take private property for public use.
ENACT - To make into a law.
ENDORSEMENT - Act of writing one's name on the back of a note, bill or similar written instrument.

ENJOIN - To require a person, by writ of injunction from a court of equity, to perform or to abstain or desist from some act.
ENTIRETY - The whole; that which the law considers as one whole, and not capable of being divided into parts.
ENTRAPMENT - Inducing one to commit a crime so as to arrest him.
ENUMERATED - Mentioned specifically; designated.
ENURE - To operate or take effect.
EQUITY - In its broadest sense, this term denotes the spirit and the habit of fairness, justness, and right dealing which regulate the conduct of men.
ERROR - A mistake of law, or the false or irregular application of law as will nullify the judicial proceedings.
ESCROW - A deed, bond or other written engagement, delivered to a third person, to be delivered by him only upon the performance or fulfillment of some condition.
ESTATE - The interest which any one has in lands, or in any other subject of property.
ESTOP - To stop, bar, or impede.
ESTOPPEL - A rule of law which prevents a man from alleging or denying a fact, because of his own previous act.
ET AL. (alii) - And others.
ET SEQ. (sequential) - And the following.
ET UX. (uxor) - And wife.
EVIDENCE - Testimony, writings, material objects, or other things presented to the senses that are offered to prove the existence or non-existence of a fact.
　　　　Means from which inferences may be drawn as a basis of proof in duly constituted judicial or fact finding tribunals, and includes testimony in the form of opinion and hearsay.
EX CONTRACTU
EX DELICTO - In law, rights and causes of action are divided into two classes, those arising *ex contractu* (from a contract) and those arising *ex delicto* (from a delict or tort).
EX OFFICIO - From office; by virtue of the office.
EX PARTE - On one side only; by or for one.
EX POST FACTO - After the fact.
EX POST FACTO LAW - A law passed after an act was done which retroactively makes such act a crime.
EX REL. (relations) - Upon relation or information.
EXCEPTION - An objection upon a matter of law to a decision made, either before or after judgment by a court.
EXECUTOR (male)
EXECUTRIX (female) - A person who has been appointed by will to execute the will.
EXECUTORY - That which is yet to be executed or performed.
EXEMPT - To release from some liability to which others are subject.
EXONERATION - The removal of a burden, charge or duty.
EXTRADITION - Surrender of a fugitive from one nation to another.

F

F.A.S.- "Free alongside ship"; delivery at dock for ship named.
F.O.B.- "Free on board"; seller will deliver to car, truck, vessel, or other conveyance by which goods are to be transported, without expense or risk of loss to the buyer or consignee.
FABRICATE - To construct; to invent a false story.
FACSIMILE - An exact or accurate copy of an original instrument.

FACTOR - A commercial agent.
FEASANCE - The doing of an act.
FELONIOUS - Criminal, malicious.
FELONY - Generally, a criminal offense that may be punished by death or imprisonment for more than one year as differentiated from a misdemeanor.
FEME SOLE - A single woman.
FIDUCIARY - A person who is invested with rights and powers to be exercised for the benefit of another person.
FIERI FACIAS - A writ of execution commanding the sheriff to levy and collect the amount of a judgment from the goods and chattels of the judgment debtor.
FINDING OF FACT - Determination from proof or judicial notice of the existence of a fact. A ruling implies a supporting finding of fact; no separate or formal finding is required unless required by a statute of this state.
FISCAL - Relating to accounts or the management of revenue.
FORECLOSURE (sale) - A sale of mortgaged property to obtain satisfaction of the mortgage out of the sale proceeds.
FORFEITURE - A penalty, a fine.
FORGERY - Fabricating or producing falsely, counterfeited.
FORTUITOUS - Accidental.
FORUM - A court of justice; a place of jurisdiction.
FRAUD - Deception; trickery.
FREEHOLDER - One who owns real property.
FUNGIBLE - Of such kind or nature that one specimen or part may be used in the place of another.

G

GARNISHEE - Person garnished.
GARNISHMENT - A legal process to reach the money or effects of a defendant, in the possession or control of a third person.
GRAND JURY - Not less than 16, not more than 23 citizens of a county sworn to inquire into crimes committed or triable in the county.
GRANT - To agree to; convey, especially real property.
GRANTEE - The person to whom a grant is made.
GRANTOR - The person by whom a grant is made.
GRATUITOUS - Given without a return, compensation or consideration.
GRAVAMEN - The grievance complained of or the substantial cause of a criminal action.
GUARANTY (n.) - A promise to answer for the payment of some debt, or the performance of some duty, in case of the failure of another person, who, in the first instance, is liable for such payment or performance.
GUARDIAN - The person, committee, or other representative authorized by law to protect the person or estate or both of an incompetent (or of a *sui juris* person having a guardian) and to act for him in matters affecting his person or property or both. An incompetent is a person under disability imposed by law.
GUILTY - Establishment of the fact that one has committed a breach of conduct; especially, a violation of law.

H

HABEAS CORPUS - You have the body; the name given to a variety of writs, having for their object to bring a party before a court or judge for decision as to whether such person is being lawfully held prisoner.

HABENDUM - In conveyancing; it is the clause in a deed conveying land which defines the extent of ownership to be held by the grantee.

HEARING - A proceeding whereby the arguments of the interested parties are heared.

HEARSAY - A type of testimony given by a witness who relates, not what he knows personally, but what others have told hi, or what he has heard said by others.

HEARSAY RULE, THE - (a) "Hearsay evidence" is evidence of a statement that was made other than by a witness while testifying at the hearing and that is offered to prove the truth of the matter stated; (b) Except as provided by law, hearsay evidence is inadmissible; (c) This section shall be known and may be cited as the hearsay rule.

HEIR - Generally, one who inherits property, real or personal.

HOLDER OF THE PRIVILEGE - (a) The client when he has no guardian or conservator; (b) A guardian or conservator of the client when the client has a guardian or conservator; (c) The personal representative of the client if the client is dead; (d) A successor, assign, trustee in dissolution, or any similar representative of a firm, association, organization, partnership, business trust, corporation, or public entity that is no longer in existence.

HUNG JURY - One so divided that they can't agree on a verdict.

HUSBAND-WIFE PRIVILEGE - An accused in a criminal proceeding has a privilege to prevent his spouse from testifying against him.

HYPOTHECATE - To pledge a thing without delivering it to the pledgee.

HYPOTHESIS - A supposition, assumption, or toehry.

I

I.E. (id est) - That is.

IB., OR IBID.(ibidem) - In the same place; used to refer to a legal reference previously cited to avoid repeating the entire citation.

ILLICIT - Prohibited; unlawful.

ILLUSORY - Deceiving by false appearance.

IMMUNITY - Exemption.

IMPEACH - To accuse, to dispute.

IMPEDIMENTS - Disabilities, or hindrances.

IMPLEAD - To sue or prosecute by due course of law.

IMPUTED - Attributed or charged to.

IN LOCO PARENTIS - In place of parent, a guardian.

IN TOTO - In the whole; completely.

INCHOATE - Imperfect; unfinished.

INCOMMUNICADO - Denial of the right of a prisoner to communicate with friends or relatives.

INCOMPETENT - One who is incapable of caring for his own affairs because he is mentally deficient or undeveloped.

INCRIMINATION - A matter will incriminate a person if it constitutes, or forms an essential part of, or, taken in connection with other matters disclosed, is a basis for a reasonable inference of such a violation of the laws of this State as to subject him to liability to punishment therefor, unless he has become for any reason permanently immune from punishment for such violation.

INCUMBRANCE - Generally a claim, lien, charge or liability attached to and binding real property.

INDEMNIFY - To secure against loss or damage; also, to make reimbursement to one for a loss already incurred by him.
INDEMNITY - An agreement to reimburse another person in case of an anticipated loss falling upon him.
INDICIA - Signs; indications.
INDICTMENT - An accusation in writing found and presented by a grand jury charging that a person has committed a crime.
INDORSE - To write a name on the back of a legal paper or document, generally, a negotiable instrument
INDUCEMENT - Cause or reason why a thing is done or that which incites the person to do the act or commit a crime; the motive for the criminal act.
INFANT - In civil cases one under 21 years of age.
INFORMATION - A formal accusation of crime made by a prosecuting attorney.
INFRA - Below, under; this word occurring by itself in a publication refers the reader to a future part of the publication.
INGRESS - The act of going into.
INJUNCTION - A writ or order by the court requiring a person, generally, to do or to refrain from doing an act.
INSOLVENT - The condition of a person who is unable to pay his debts.
INSTRUCTION - A direction given by the judge to the jury concerning the law of the case.
INTERIM - In the meantime; time intervening.
INTERLOCUTORY - Temporary, not final; something intervening between the commencement and the end of a suit which decides some point or matter, but is not a final decision of the whole controversy.
INTERROGATORIES - A series of formal written questions used in the examination of a party or a witness usually prior to a trial.
INTESTATE - A person who dies without a will.
INURE - To result, to take effect.
IPSO FACTO - By the fact iself; by the mere fact.
ISSUE (n.) The disputed point or question in a case,

J

JEOPARDY - Danger, hazard, peril.
JOINDER - Joining; uniting with another person in some legal steps or proceeding.
JOINT - United; combined.
JUDGE - Member or members or representative or representatives of a court conducting a trial or hearing at which evidence is introduced.
JUDGMENT - The official decision of a court of justice.
JUDICIAL OR JUDICIARY - Relating to or connected with the administration of justice.
JURAT - The clause written at the foot of an affidavit, stating when, where and before whom such affidavit was sworn.
JURISDICTION - The authority to hear and determine controversies between parties.
JURISPRUDENCE - The philosophy of law.
JURY - A body of persons legally selected to inquire into any matter of fact, and to render their verdict according to the evidence.

L

LACHES - The failure to diligently assert a right, which results in a refusal to allow relief.

LANDLORD AND TENANT - A phrase used to denote the legal relation existing between the owner and occupant of real estate.
LARCENY - Stealing personal property belonging to another.
LATENT - Hidden; that which does not appear on the face of a thing.
LAW - Includes constitutional, statutory, and decisional law.
LAWYER-CLIENT PRIVILEGE - (1) A "client" is a person, public officer, or corporation, association, or other organization or entity, either public or private, who is rendered professional legal services by a lawyer, or who consults a lawyer with a view to obtaining professional legal services from him; (2) A "lawyer" is a person authorized, or reasonably believed by the client to be authorized, to practice law in any state or nation; (3) A "representative of the lawyer" is one employed to assist the lawyer in the rendition of professional legal services; (4) A communication is "confidential" if not intended to be disclosed to third persons other than those to whom disclosure is in furtherance of the rendition of professional legal services to the client or those reasonably necessary for the transmission of the communication.

General rule of privilege - A client has a privilege to refuse to disclose and to prevent any other person from disclosing confidential communications made for the purpose of facilitating the rendition of professional legal services to the client, (1) between himself or his representative and his lawyer or his lawyer's representative, or (2) between his lawyer and the lawyer's representative, or (3) by him or his lawyer to a lawyer representing another in a matter of common interest, or (4) between representatives of the client or between the client and a representative of the client, or (5) between lawyers representing the client.

LEADING QUESTION - Question that suggests to the witness the answer that the examining party desires.
LEASE - A contract by which one conveys real estate for a limited time usually for a specified rent; personal property also may be leased.
LEGISLATION - The act of enacting laws.
LEGITIMATE - Lawful.
LESSEE - One to whom a lease is given.
LESSOR - One who grants a lease
LEVY - A collecting or exacting by authority.
LIABLE - Responsible; bound or obligated in law or equity.
LIBEL (v.) - To defame or injure a person's reputation by a published writing.
 (n.) - The initial pleading on the part of the plaintiff in an admiralty proceeding.
LIEN - A hold or claim which one person has upon the property of another as a security for some debt or charge.
LIQUIDATED - Fixed; settled.
LIS PENDENS - A pending civil or criminal action.
LITERAL - According to the language.
LITIGANT - A party to a lawsuit.
LITATION - A judicial controversy.
LOCUS - A place.
LOCUS DELICTI - Place of the crime.
LOCUS POENITENTIAE - The abandoning or giving up of one's intention to commit some crime before it is fully completed or abandoning a conspiracy before its purpose is accomplished.

M

MALFEASANCE - To do a wrongful act.
MALICE - The doing of a wrongful act Intentionally without just cause or excuse.

MANDAMUS - The name of a writ issued by a court to enforce the performance of some public duty.
MANDATORY (adj.) Containing a command.
MARITIME - Pertaining to the sea or to commerce thereon.
MARSHALING - Arranging or disposing of in order.
MAXIM - An established principle or proposition.
MINISTERIAL - That which involves obedience to instruction, but demands no special discretion, judgment or skill.
MISAPPROPRIATE - Dealing fraudulently with property entrusted to one.
MISDEMEANOR - A crime less than a felony and punishable by a fine or imprisonment for less than one year.
MISFEASANCE - Improper performance of a lawful act.
MISREPRESENTATION - An untrue representation of facts.
MITIGATE - To make or become less severe, harsh.
MITTIMUS - A warrant of commitment to prison.
MOOT (adj.) Unsettled, undecided, not necessary to be decided.
MORTGAGE - A conveyance of property upon condition, as security for the payment of a debt or the performance of a duty, and to become void upon payment or performance according to the stipulated terms.
MORTGAGEE - A person to whom property is mortgaged.
MORTGAGOR - One who gives a mortgage.
MOTION - In legal proceedings, a "motion" is an application, either written or oral, addressed to the court by a party to an action or a suit requesting the ruling of the court on a matter of law.
MUTUALITY - Reciprocation.

N

NEGLIGENCE - The failure to exercise that degree of care which an ordinarily prudent person would exercise under like circumstances.
NEGOTIABLE (instrument) - Any instrument obligating the payment of money which is transferable from one person to another by endorsement and delivery or by delivery only.
NEGOTIATE - To transact business; to transfer a negotiable instrument; to seek agreement for the amicable disposition of a controversy or case.
NOLLE PROSEQUI - A formal entry upon the record, by the plaintiff in a civil suit or the prosecuting officer in a criminal action, by which he declares that he "will no further prosecute" the case.
NOLO CONTENDERE - The name of a plea in a criminal action, having the same effect as a plea of guilty; but not constituting a direct admission of guilt.
NOMINAL - Not real or substantial.
NOMINAL DAMAGES - Award of a trifling sum where no substantial injury is proved to have been sustained.
NONFEASANCE - Neglect of duty.
NOVATION - The substitution of a new debt or obligation for an existing one.
NUNC PRO TUNC - A phrase applied to acts allowed to be done after the time when they should be done, with a retroactive effect.("Now for then.")

O

OATH - Oath includes affirmation or declaration under penalty of perjury.
OBITER DICTUM - Opinion expressed by a court on a matter not essentially involved in a case and hence not a decision; also called dicta, if plural.

OBJECT (v.) - To oppose as improper or illegal and referring the question of its propriety or legality to the court.
OBLIGATION - A legal duty, by which a person is bound to do or not to do a certain thing.
OBLIGEE - The person to whom an obligation is owed.
OBLIGOR - The person who is to perform the obligation.
OFFER (v.) - To present for acceptance or rejection.
(n.) - A proposal to do a thing, usually a proposal to make a contract.
OFFICIAL INFORMATION - Information within the custody or control of a department or agency of the government the disclosure of which is shown to be contrary to the public interest.
OFFSET - A deduction.
ONUS PROBANDI - Burden of proof.
OPINION - The statement by a judge of the decision reached in a case, giving the law as applied to the case and giving reasons for the judgment; also a belief or view.
OPTION - The exercise of the power of choice; also a privilege existing in one person, for which he has paid money, which gives him the right to buy or sell real or personal property at a given price within a specified time.
ORDER - A rule or regulation; every direction of a court or judge made or entered in writing but not including a judgment.
ORDINANCE - Generally, a rule established by authority; also commonly used to designate the legislative acts of a municipal corporation.
ORIGINAL - Writing or recording itself or any counterpart intended to have the same effect by a person executing or issuing it. An "original" of a photograph includes the negative or any print therefrom. If data are stored in a computer or similar device, any printout or other output readable by sight, shown to reflect the data accurately, is an "original."
OVERT - Open, manifest.

P

PANEL - A group of jurors selected to serve during a term of the court.
PARENS PATRIAE - Sovereign power of a state to protect or be a guardian over children and incompetents.
PAROL - Oral or verbal.
PAROLE - To release one in prison before the expiration of his sentence, conditionally.
PARITY - Equality in purchasing power between the farmer and other segments of the economy.
PARTITION - A legal division of real or personal property between one or more owners.
PARTNERSHIP - An association of two or more persons to carry on as co-owners a business for profit.
PATENT (adj.) - Evident.
(n.) - A grant of some privilege, property, or authority, made by the government or sovereign of a country to one or more individuals.
PECULATION - Stealing.
PECUNIARY - Monetary.
PENULTIMATE - Next to the last.
PER CURIAM - A phrase used in the report of a decision to distinguish an opinion of the whole court from an opinion written by any one judge.
PER SE - In itself; taken alone.
PERCEIVE - To acquire knowledge through one's senses.
PEREMPTORY - Imperative; absolute.
PERJURY - To lie or state falsely under oath.

PERPETUITY - Perpetual existence; also the quality or condition of an estate limited so that it will not take effect or vest within the period fixed by law.
PERSON - Includes a natural person, firm, association, organization, partnership, business trust, corporation, or public entity.
PERSONAL PROPERTY - Includes money, goods, chattels, things in action, and evidences of debt.
PERSONALTY - Short term for personal property.
PETITION - An application in writing for an order of the court, stating the circumstances upon which it is founded and requesting any order or other relief from a court.
PLAINTIFF - A person who brings a court action.
PLEA - A pleading in a suit or action.
PLEADINGS - Formal allegations made by the parties of their respective claims and defenses, for the judgment of the court.
PLEDGE - A deposit of personal property as a security for the performance of an act.
PLEDGEE - The party to whom goods are delivered in pledge.
PLEDGOR - The party delivering goods in pledge.
PLENARY - Full; complete.
POLICE POWER - Inherent power of the state or its political subdivisions to enact laws within constitutional limits to promote the general welfare of society or the community.
POLLING THE JURY - Call the names of persons on a jury and requiring each juror to declare what his verdict is before it is legally recorded.
POST MORTEM - After death.
POWER OF ATTORNEY - A writing authorizing one to act for another.
PRECEPT - An order, warrant, or writ issued to an officer or body of officers, commanding him or them to do some act within the scope of his or their powers.
PRELIMINARY FACT - Fact upon the existence or nonexistence of which depends the admissibility or inadmissibility of evidence. The phrase "the admissibility or inadmissibility of evidence" includes the qualification or disqualification of a person to be a witness and the existence or nonexistence of a privilege.
PREPONDERANCE - Outweighing.
PRESENTMENT - A report by a grand jury on something they have investigated on their own knowledge.
PRESUMPTION - An assumption of fact resulting from a rule of law which requires such fact to be assumed from another fact or group of facts found or otherwise established in the action.
PRIMA FACUE - At first sight.
PRIMA FACIE CASE - A case where the evidence is very patent against the defendant.
PRINCIPAL - The source of authority or rights; a person primarily liable as differentiated from "principle" as a primary or basic doctrine.
PRO AND CON - For and against.
PRO RATA - Proportionally.
PROBATE - Relating to proof, especially to the proof of wills.
PROBATIVE - Tending to prove.
PROCEDURE - In law, this term generally denotes rules which are established by the Federal, State, or local Governments regarding the types of pleading and courtroom practice which must be followed by the parties involved in a criminal or civil case.
PROCLAMATION - A public notice by an official of some order, intended action, or state of facts.

PROFFERED EVIDENCE - The admissibility or inadmissibility of which is dependent upon the existence or nonexistence of a preliminary fact.

PROMISSORY (NOTE) - A promise in writing to pay a specified sum at an expressed time, or on demand, or at sight, to a named person, or to his order, or bearer.

PROOF - The establishment by evidence of a requisite degree of belief concerning a fact in the mind of the trier of fact or the court.

PROPERTY - Includes both real and personal property.

PROPRIETARY (adj.) - Relating or pertaining to ownership; usually a single owner.

PROSECUTE - To carry on an action or other judicial proceeding; to proceed against a person criminally.

PROVISO - A limitation or condition in a legal instrument.

PROXIMATE - Immediate; nearest

PUBLIC EMPLOYEE - An officer, agent, or employee of a public entity.

PUBLIC ENTITY - Includes a national, state, county, city and county, city, district, public authority, public agency, or any other political subdivision or public corporation, whether foreign or domestic.

PUBLIC OFFICIAL - Includes an official of a political dubdivision of such state or territory and of a municipality.

PUNITIVE - Relating to punishment.

Q

QUASH - To make void.

QUASI - As if; as it were.

QUID PRO QUO - Something for something; the giving of one valuable thing for another.

QUITCLAIM (v.) - To release or relinquish claim or title to, especially in deeds to realty.

QUO WARRANTO - A legal procedure to test an official's right to a public office or the right to hold a franchise, or to hold an office in a domestic corporation.

R

RATIFY - To approve and sanction.

REAL PROPERTY - Includes lands, tenements, and hereditaments.

REALTY - A brief term for real property.

REBUT - To contradict; to refute, especially by evidence and arguments.

RECEIVER - A person who is appointed by the court to receive, and hold in trust property in litigation.

RECIDIVIST - Habitual criminal.

RECIPROCAL - Mutual.

RECOUPMENT - To keep back or get something which is due; also, it is the right of a defendant to have a deduction from the amount of the plaintiff's damages because the plaintiff has not fulfilled his part of the same contract.

RECROSS EXAMINATION - Examination of a witness by a cross-examiner subsequent to a redirect examination of the witness.

REDEEM - To release an estate or article from mortgage or pledge by paying the debt for which it stood as security.

REDIRECT EXAMINATION - Examination of a witness by the direct examiner subsequent to the cross-examination of the witness.

REFEREE - A person to whom a cause pending in a court is referred by the court, to take testimony, hear the parties, and report thereon to the court.

REFERENDUM - A method of submitting an important legislative or administrative matter to a direct vote of the people.
RELEVANT EVIDENCE - Evidence including evidence relevant to the credulity of a witness or hearsay declarant, having any tendency in reason to prove or disprove any disputed fact that is of consequence to the determination of the action.
REMAND - To send a case back to the lower court from which it came, for further proceedings.
REPLEVIN - An action to recover goods or chattels wrongfully taken or detained.
REPLY (REPLICATION) - Generally, a reply is what the plaintiff or other person who has instituted proceedings says in answer to the defendant's case.
RE JUDICATA - A thing judicially acted upon or decided.
RES ADJUDICATA - Doctrine that an issue or dispute litigated and determined in a case between the opposing parties is deemed permanently decided between these parties.
RESCIND (RECISSION) - To avoid or cancel a contract.
RESPONDENT - A defendant in a proceeding in chancery or admiralty; also, the person who contends against the appeal in a case.
RESTITUTION - In equity, it is the restoration of both parties to their original condition (when practicable), upon the rescission of a contract for fraud or similar cause.
RETROACTIVE (RETROSPECTIVE) - Looking back; effective as of a prior time.
REVERSED - A term used by appellate courts to indicate that the decision of the lower court in the case before it has been set aside.
REVOKE - To recall or cancel.
RIPARIAN (RIGHTS) - The rights of a person owning land containing or bordering on a water course or other body of water, such as lakes and rivers.

S

SALE - A contract whereby the ownership of property is transferred from one person to another for a sum of money or for any consideration.
SANCTION - A penalty or punishment provided as a means of enforcing obedience to a law; also, an authorization.
SATISFACTION - The discharge of an obligation by paying a party what is due to him; or what is awarded to him by the judgment of a court or otherwise.
SCIENTER - Knowingly; also, it is used in pleading to denote the defendant's guilty knowledge.
SCINTILLA - A spark; also the least particle.
SECRET OF STATE - Governmental secret relating to the national defense or the international relations of the United States.
SECURITY - Indemnification; the term is applied to an obligation, such as a mortgage or deed of trust, given by a debtor to insure the payment or performance of his debt, by furnishing the creditor with a resource to be used in case of the debtor's failure to fulfill the principal obligation.
SENTENCE - The judgment formally pronounced by the court or judge upon the defendant after his conviction in a criminal prosecution.
SET-OFF - A claim or demand which one party in an action credits against the claim of the opposing party.
SHALL and MAY - "Shall" is mandatory and "may" is permissive.
SITUS - Location.
SOVEREIGN - A person, body or state in which independent and supreme authority is vested.
STARE DECISIS - To follow decided cases.

STATE - "State" means this State, unless applied to the different parts of the United States. In the latter case, it includes any state, district, commonwealth, territory or insular possession of the United States, including the District of Columbia.

STATEMENT - (a) Oral or written verbal expression or (b) nonverbal conduct of a person intended by him as a substitute for oral or written verbal expression.

STATUTE - An act of the legislature. Includes a treaty.

STATUTE OF LIMITATION - A statute limiting the time to bring an action after the right of action has arisen.

STAY - To hold in abeyance an order of a court.

STIPULATION - Any agreement made by opposing attorneys regulating any matter incidental to the proceedings or trial.

SUBORDINATION (AGREEMENT) - An agreement making one's rights inferior to or of a lower rank than another's.

SUBORNATION - The crime of procuring a person to lie or to make false statements to a court.

SUBPOENA - A writ or order directed to a person, and requiring his attendance at a particular time and place to testify as a witness.

SUBPOENA DUCES TECUM - A subpoena used, not only for the purpose of compelling witnesses to attend in court, but also requiring them to bring with them books or documents which may be in their possession, and which may tend to elucidate the subject matter of the trial.

SUBROGATION - The substituting of one for another as a creditor, the new creditor succeeding to the former's rights.

SUBSIDY - A government grant to assist a private enterprise deemed advantageous to the public.

SUI GENERIS - Of the same kind.

SUIT - Any civil proceeding by a person or persons against another or others in a court of justice by which the plaintiff pursues the remedies afforded him by law.

SUMMONS - A notice to a defendant that an action against him has been commenced and requiring him to appear in court and answer the complaint.

SUPRA - Above; this word occurring by itself in a book refers the reader to a previous part of the book.

SURETY - A person who binds himself for the payment of a sum of money, or for the performance of something else, for another.

SURPLUSAGE - Extraneous or unnecessary matter.

SURVIVORSHIP - A term used when a person becomes entitled to property by reason of his having survived another person who had an interest in the property.

SUSPEND SENTENCE - Hold back a sentence pending good behavior of prisoner.

SYLLABUS - A note prefixed to a report, especially a case, giving a brief statement of the court's ruling on different issues of the case.

T

TALESMAN - Person summoned to fill a panel of jurors.

TENANT - One who holds or possesses lands by any kind of right or title; also, one who has the temporary use and occupation of real property owned by another person (landlord), the duration and terms of his tenancy being usually fixed by an instrument called "a lease."

TENDER - An offer of money; an expression of willingness to perform a contract according to its terms.

TERM - When used with reference to a court, it signifies the period of time during which the court holds a session, usually of several weeks or months duration.

TESTAMENTARY - Pertaining to a will or the administration of a will.
TESTATOR (male)
TESTATRIX (female) - One who makes or has made a testament or will.
TESTIFY (TESTIMONY) - To give evidence under oath as a witness.
TO WIT - That is to say; namely.
TORT - Wrong; injury to the person.
TRANSITORY - Passing from place to place.
TRESPASS - Entry into another's ground, illegally.
TRIAL - The examination of a cause, civil or criminal, before a judge who has jurisdiction over it, according to the laws of the land.
TRIER OF FACT - Includes (a) the jury and (b) the court when the court is trying an issue of fact other than one relating to the admissibility of evidence.
TRUST - A right of property, real or personal, held by one party for the benefit of another.
TRUSTEE - One who lawfully holds property in custody for the benefit of another.

U

UNAVAILABLE AS A WITNESS - The declarant is (1) Exempted or precluded on the ground of privilege from testifying concerning the matter to which his statement is relevant; (2) Disqualified from testifying to the matter; (3) Dead or unable to attend or to testify at the hearing because of then existing physical or mental illness or infirmity; (4) Absent from the hearing and the court is unable to compel his attendance by its process; or (5) Absent from the hearing and the proponent of his statement has exercised reasonable diligence but has been unable to procure his attendance by the court's process.
ULTRA VIRES - Acts beyond the scope and power of a corporation, association, etc.
UNILATERAL - One-sided; obligation upon, or act of one party.
USURY - Unlawful interest on a loan.

V

VACATE - To set aside; to move out.
VARIANCE - A discrepancy or disagreement between two instruments or two aspects of the same case, which by law should be consistent.
VENDEE - A purchaser or buyer.
VENDOR - The person who transfers property by sale, particularly real estate; the term "seller" is used more commonly for one who sells personal property.
VENIREMEN - Persons ordered to appear to serve on a jury or composing a panel of jurors.
VENUE - The place at which an action is tried, generally based on locality or judicial district in which an injury occurred or a material fact happened.
VERDICT - The formal decision or finding of a jury.
VERIFY - To confirm or substantiate by oath.
VEST - To accrue to.
VOID - Having no legal force or binding effect.
VOIR DIRE - Preliminary examination of a witness or a juror to test competence, interest, prejudice, etc.

W

WAIVE - To give up a right.
WAIVER - The intentional or voluntary relinquishment of a known right.
WARRANT (WARRANTY) (v.) - To promise that a certain fact or state of facts, in relation to the subject matter, is, or shall be, as it is represented to be.

WARRANT (n.) - A writ issued by a judge, or other competent authority, addressed to a sheriff, or other officer, requiring him to arrest the person therein named, and bring him before the judge or court to answer or be examined regarding the offense with which he is charged.

WRIT - An order or process issued in the name of the sovereign or in the name of a court or judicial officer, commanding the performance or nonperformance of some act.

WRITING - Handwriting, typewriting, printing, photostating, photographing and every other means of recording upon any tangible thing any form of communication or representation, including letters, words, pictures, sounds, or symbols, or combinations thereof.

WRITINGS AND RECORDINGS - Consists of letters, words, or numbers, or their equivalent, set down by handwriting, typewriting, printing, photostating, photographing, magnetic impulse, mechanical or electronic recording, or other form of data compilation.

Y

YEA AND NAY - Yes and no.

YELLOW DOG CONTRACT - A contract by which employer requires employee to sign an instrument promising as condition that he will not join a union during its continuance, and will be discharged if he does join.

Z

ZONING - The division of a city by legislative regulation into districts and the prescription and application in each district of regulations having to do with structural and architectural designs of buildings and of regulations prescribing use to which buildings within designated districts may be put.

www.ingramcontent.com/pod-product-compliance
Lightning Source LLC
Chambersburg PA
CBHW081820300426
44116CB00014B/2425